Spies Who Never Were

By the same author

SPY MYSTERIES UNVEILED

COLONEL VERNON HINCHLEY

Spies
Who Never
Were

DODD, MEAD & COMPANY
New York

Contents

ONE

Who are the Spies?

I

NO SUBJECT SO PERVERTS THE TRUTH as does espionage. Falsehood is an essential feature of the spy's trade, and 'official' accounts of the career and trial of an unsuccessful agent are invariably misleading. Add the ingenious methods employed by the sensational Press—especially in some foreign countries—by which details are perverted and exaggerated, and within a few years a legend develops which bears little or no relation to the basic record.

Rumour is apt to be born of or develop into untruth. How many people in Britain during the Second World War heard "Lord Haw-Haw" broadcast about the eccentricities of the local town-hall or church clock, thus implying that the district was permeated with German spies! Haw-Haw *never* mentioned anybody's clock!

According to rumours then prevalent, German spies were everywhere: they usually operated radio-sets up their chimneys. But at no point in either World War were there more than two spies simultaneously at large in Britain. Even the Germans made fun. I remember a cartoon in a German magazine in 1914. It showed a dachshund being

7

arrested by a large force of London police. "Dirty German
spy!" roared the crowd. "Caught signalling to a Zeppelin
with his tail." The climax showed the badger-hound, his
eyes bandaged, facing a firing-squad in the Tower.

Rumour is today part of the spy's trade, for its results
can be as devastating as any feat of military espionage.
But is a rumour-monger a spy? If so, countless thousands of people have been guilty of treachery to their own
countries.

Was Nurse Cavell a spy? She never engaged in espionage,
but she nursed British and Belgian soldiers and smuggled
them out of German-occupied Belgium: highly repre-
hensible from the German viewpoint, doubtless, but scarcely deserving of a spy's death at the hands of a firing-squad.

Or consider the case of M. E. Clifton-James, who has
often been quite wrongly dubbed a spy.

He was an actor, and bore a remarkable resemblance to
Field-Marshal Montgomery. One night, at a troops concert,
he gave an amazingly accurate 'impression' of Monty; he
had caught his mannerisms, tricks of speech, and idiosyn-
crasies. The troops loved it, and it gave an Intelligence
officer who was present an idea: the Intelligence officer was
David Niven, the actor.

Clifton-James was quietly withdrawn from his unit, and
began a special training—a study of Monty, carefully watching how he walked, talked, and looked on a variety of
occasions.

Then, after one or two try-outs, he left at the end of
May 1944 for Gibraltar—*as* Monty. He received the full
V.I.P. treatment, guards of honour and all, talked with
Monty's confidence to staff officers, and inspected the
troops of the garrison. His impersonation was perfect.

Now thousands of Spanish workmen crossed from La Linea into Gibraltar every day to work in the dockyard or town. The great majority were intensely loyal—had worked in Gib. all their lives. But it would have been amazing if the Germans had not infiltrated a few spies among them.

These men duly reported Monty's presence—and were, of course, believed. The dumbest spy could scarcely make a mistake about Monty!

So the German staff was thoroughly deceived. The Allied landing in France was being expected almost every day. Obviously the attack would never be launched while Monty was at Gibraltar! So the Germans relaxed—to get a great surprise when the Allied force, under Monty's own command, landed on the Normandy beaches.

Admirable Intelligence work, but nothing to do with espionage.

A spy trial, I said, can be misleading. It is usually held *in camera*, and an official announcement gives only the bare bones of the case. The 'whole truth' is an essential feature of British justice, and applies to the trial of a spy—but *not* to the later official version. The restraint is comprehensible: details of the method by which the spy was caught might warn other spies; or notes on his activities might aid the enemy in evaluating his information.

The classic case of the spy-who-never-was formed the basis for my selection: Captain Alfred Dreyfus. His record appears early in this book—if only as a warning that such things can happen in a civilized country. They can happen *anywhere*. Captain Dreyfus was sentenced to lifelong imprisonment by a French military court-martial, but Mrs O'Grady was sentenced *to death* by a British judge after trial by the civilian code.

The cases I have selected as examples cover a dozen countries. Some are well known—that of Alger Hiss promises to be classed as the Dreyfus case of our time—others may be almost unknown to the general reader, but do not lose anything in drama because of that.

Were the members of the French Resistance spies? It is not a crime for a man to defend his own country, and for that a rifle is much more important than a uniform. Yet the lack of this gave the Nazis the excuse for executing their captives on trumped-up charges of espionage.

This war-time overlapping of Intelligence and Resistance —roughly speaking, the passive and active branches of secret work inside enemy countries—has given Whitehall many a hard problem. The Germans started the War with their Abwehr—the old professional Secret Service—sensibly and practically organized into Division I for espionage and Division III for sabotage. But when the Nazis eliminated the Abwehr chief Admiral Canaris they confused the functions of the two branches and failed dismally at both.

Britain had foreseen these dangers from the start. The permanent establishment of MI6—commonly called the Foreign Secret Service—was never allowed to overlap, or even to co-operate, with the war-time SOE, the Special Operations Executive, which organized resistance and sabotage in enemy-occupied countries, "to set Europe aflame", as Sir Winston Churchill put it in an unforgettable phrase.

British policy led to the occasional need for some heart-rending decisions. When a MI6 man posing as, say, a Gestapo officer found himself investigating the activities of a compatriot whom he knew to be a SOE agent, should he earn promotion from his German superiors and thus become a still more valuable source of information to his country? Or should he jeopardize his hard-won position in the enemy camp by obeying his natural impulse to help a fellow-countryman? Such stories may not yet be told. But they account for certain nightmares which haunt the minds of retired spies. Does the end justify the means? Who shall ever decide?

This is not a book on psychology. But it can be briefly stated that the basic British policy in selecting officers and agents for secret work in enemy territory was almost identical with that of the Royal Air Force in selecting its pilots. Introverts were chosen for MI6 and as bomber-pilots, forging relentlessly ahead to their objective regardless of what was happening around them. Extroverts were chosen for SOE and as fighter-pilots, recklessly ranging the skies with a roving commission to find and kill the enemy.

The problem is not by any means a new one. One of Britain's most brilliant spies was Sidney Reilly. But towards the end of his career his hatred of Communism impelled him in the direction of active anti-Soviet activities in Russia. He would probably have been of much more use to Britain if he had continued in his rôle of a Soviet commissar and sent back information to Whitehall.

A somewhat similar case is that of Colonel T. E. Lawrence. He too started off in Intelligence work, his knowledge of the Middle East and of the Arabic language qualifying him for a useful if unglamorous job in the map-room of British Military Headquarters in Cairo. Like Reilly, Lawrence eventually went out into enemy country—Arabia then being territory belonging to Turkey, with whom Britain was at war. And, like Reilly, he became a convert to the cause of the people among whom he was working. Unlike Reilly, however,

Lawrence was probably much more useful sabotaging Tur-
kish railways than if he had remained among his maps in
Cairo.

II

One evening late in 1939 I was in the bar of the famous
Lion d'Or in Rheims in the company of a senior R.A.F.
officer. A man near by was apparently determined to get
into our conversation.

He proved to be the business manager of a visiting concert
party. But this, he confided to us, was only a cover: he was
actually an important member of the British Secret Service.
He went on to recount some of his exploits, which were
quite remarkable. Noticing our interest, he proceeded to
describe feats of espionage far more reminiscent of James
Bond than of real life. The joke was that at that time I was
'official', and my companion was Intelligence Officer to the
Advanced Air Striking Force.

The man was just a fool—an insignificant and pathetic
fellow, avid for publicity. We let him down very lightly—but
the concert party continued its tour of the camps short of a
manager.

He was one of a very numerous type. The pose of the
Secret Service man is much favoured: it implies outstanding
courage and ingenuity. Psychologists explain that such people
have usually suffered from a compulsive neurosis, often aggra-
vated by childhood frustrations or disciplines, or by sexual
frustrations and a sterile marriage. It involves a genuinely
diminished sense of responsibility linked to a facile imagination; and an underlying, basic immaturity.

There is no end to these cases, which are encountered in
almost every country. One recently made headlines in the

British Press. A man retired from the Navy had a threefold 'career'. He was a British spy, and produced some official papers marked "Secret" at a crucial point in his story. Or he was a Russian agent: or, alternatively, a daredevil who boasted that he was open to the highest bidder for any job from spying to killing—pistol produced. He was experienced in all three genres, including killing, he claimed.

He was as unlucky as the concert-party manager. A young couple met him in a London coffee bar. He spoke with a thick foreign accent, and began his recital. He was an "international agent", who would "sell anything to anyone as long as the price is right". Later he indulged in the remainder of his repertoire.

His name, he said, was Nikolai Bryanovitch Petrov. But by an extraordinary chance one of his confidants spoke Russian fluently; and, as Bryanovitch is a name unknown in the Slav countries, he was put on his guard. When the 'spy' got as far as his 'Secret' papers—they were genuine: he had wrongly retained them when he left the Navy—his audience had the sense to take him to the nearest police-station. The impostor was lucky to escape with a modest fine.

Cases crop up now and again in peace-time of what the newspapers headline as "Bogus MI5 Major" or something similar. The offences are usually that a plausible charlatan has told a romantic story to impress and later swindle an unsuspecting woman. Actually the official policy is to turn a blind eye to such people, so long as they restrict their activities to mere boasting, which does nobody any harm. It may even, in fact, help the Security authorities!

During the War, for instance, there was a steady trickle of reports from all over Britain of men who frequented expensive saloon bars and muttered in phoney public-school

accents that they were officers of the British Secret Service.
This usually procured them free drinks from suckers who
were excited by the feeling of 'being in the know'. The
official attitude is summarized by a minute in a certain secret
file: "No action on this man. By parading the West End in a
blaze of secrecy he is likely to attract and divert the attention
of genuine foreign agents, while we get on with our job."

A case in which something did have to be done was when
the nervous wife of an elderly man living in a London
suburb complained to the authorities. "Don't you think my
husband is doing enough for his country?" she wrote. "He
works hard all day, and two evenings a week he drills with
the local Home Guard. So why should you expect him to do
dangerous work on three other nights a week as a member of
the Home Guard Secret Service? I know it's dangerous
because he has to go out at nights in plain clothes and take
his Home Guard bayonet for protection against enemy spies."

The facts were that after a lifetime of dull domesticity
the husband realized what fun it could be to have a few
drinks with colleagues after a Home Guard parade. So,
using Home Guard duties as an excuse—and he was not by
any means the only one!—he escaped from his unexciting
home life on several other evenings every week, but with no
excuse for not wearing his uniform except his 'Secret Service'
yarn. But he tried to be too clever. He thought that by
letting his wife know that he was carrying his bayonet—
an inadequate defence against a spy's Luger—he would
be providing what W. S. Gilbert calls in *The Mikado*
"corroborative detail, intended to give artistic verisimilitude
to an otherwise bald and unconvincing narrative". The result
was that his unfortunate wife was scared to death, and the
'local' lost a promising member of its darts team.

Boasts by immature exhibitionists, with espionage as a favourite theme, are common enough. But there are men who should know better, among them journalists who write books of the 'scissors-and-paste' variety which are consistently inaccurate: true, it is easy to be misled, and easier to mislead yourself, in a record of espionage.

But others are sheer deceivers. They usually pose as ex-spies, and their adventures are amazing. If they were true the Official Secrets Act would be overworked: but MI5 is not interested in fiction.

Yet most of these 'ex-spies' fell into the same trap. Fascinated by the story of Mata Hari, they usually introduced her into their adventures. Some had spied with her: others had slept with her—a few had done both. They quoted freely from her own legendary exploits as a guarantee of their own veracity. Unfortunately for them, they never attempted to check the story as popularly accepted—which has no foundation of fact.

I have one book written by a self-confessed "international spy".[1] He wrote under his code number 'E.7', and achieved some publicity from the BBC and other reputable bodies early in the last war. He had known Mata Hari well, so he said. He had spent a holiday with her in Java in 1905— he is sure of the date. But she left Java in 1902, never to return.

His story bristles with such mistakes of detail. It culminated in 1910, when he accompanied Mata Hari to the U.S.A. —to steal the plans of a naval "death-ray" which could produce an explosion thirty miles away.

Their mission was successful. Mata Hari seduced a senior American officer and retired with the plans tucked under her corsets. E.7 excitedly records that as a result of this device the

[1] *Women Spies I have Known*, by 'E.7'.

Germans sank the British battle-cruisers at the battle of Jutland.

E.7 should indeed have followed the old journalistic advice: "Check, check, and then verify". His story shrieks with falsehoods and fantasy. (1) The battle-cruisers were sunk by much more mundane methods than a death-ray—by good German shooting coupled with serious faults in their design. (2) The Americans have never heard of their naval death-ray. (3) If E.7 had helped to supply the Germans with a device which sank the battle-cruisers, why was he not arrested, tried, and condemned? (4) I have traced from Mata Hari's Press-cutting album that she was dancing in Europe throughout the whole of 1910. (5) She *never* went to America in all her life!

A more innocent but still rather deceptive form of entertainment (for it is nothing more) formed the basis of the popular radio and TV series of Colonel Oreste Pinto, the "Spy-catcher". He appears conducting interrogations of suspected spies, which by virtue of his knowledge of languages he carried out quite efficiently during the War at the Royal Patriotic School at Wandsworth.

But "Spy-catcher" is a singularly inapposite title. Anyone with any Security sense will realize that the faceless men who actually catch spies hardly ever appear as interrogators or as witnesses, lest their identities become known and their value diminish.

In very exceptional cases the importance of breaking up a foreign spy-ring justifies calling 'watcher' witnesses, as in the Lonsdale case. They are the real spy-catchers, not Army officers who sit in remote offices asking a prearranged list of questions. But such witnesses, officially recorded as "Mr A", "Miss B", and so on, are picked as inconspicuous types, and I defy any observant journalist who saw them in court to attempt to give any personal description of them that might help a potential enemy to identify them as Secret Service agents.

III

Some serious and knowledgeable people actually believe that Admiral Canaris, head of the German Secret Service during the last war, was a British spy!

Canaris was no Teuton: he came of Italian stock, and had the imagination of the Latins. His hobby was peculiar: he was an excellent amateur cook, and loved to entertain guests with dishes of his own concoction. Though a brilliant spy-master, he was in private life kindly and with a keen sense of humour. So he was unlikely to be enamoured of a humourless and brutal character like Adolf Hitler. He was, in fact, one of the few who were proof against Hitler's mesmeric personality.

Canaris had a similar hypnotic quality. When Hitler flew into a rage which scared his tough generals the little admiral could always soothe him. He himself had his own troubles— in the Nazi spy organizations set up as rivals to his own.

In 1944 the local Abwehr chief in Turkey defected to the British—to whom he gave a remarkably complete account of German Secret Service organization. Himmler, head of the Gestapo, had long been jealous of Canaris. He took advantage of Hitler's frenzied rage to blame Canaris for the disaster. After long torture the admiral was hanged—by a piece of piano wire!

He had never been a traitor: true, he hated Hitler and admired Britain—especially the Royal Navy, from whose traditions the German Navy had freely borrowed. But there was no evidence whatsoever that he was a British spy. He

B

did a sound professional job for his own country, as was his
duty, and his hate of the Nazi regime did not transform him
into a traitor.

Other men have been charged with espionage from a very
different angle. After the death of Stalin in 1953 the control
of Russia was assumed by a triumvirate 'collective leadership'
of G. M. Malenkov, V. M. Molotov, and L. P. Beria. The
last-named held the powerful post of chief of police—
including the secret police.

Suddenly he himself was arrested, on a charge that he had
plotted against the Communist Party and Government, and
that he was an American spy!

This story was, of course, as fantastic as any of the imagin-
ings of E.7. But this pattern was rigidly followed in all the
Communist countries during the anti-Stalinist shocks. Lifelong Communists, who had risen to the highest rank in their
own countries, were executed as American spies: or occasionally, for a change, as British spies. True, most of them
were later rehabilitated, but we were led to believe that at
one period most of the Communist countries were governed
by American or British spies!

The suggestion is quite absurd, and I do not propose to
waste further space on it.

IV

I was tempted to include in my book the records of some
men who really were spies, but not as they were reputed to
be. One example must, however, suffice.

The newly restored Poland was understandably nervous of
her German neighbour, and in 1925 Captain Jerzy (George)
Sosnowski was sent to Berlin as a spy. His cover was unusual:

he was a first-class horseman, and now proposed to race his horses in Germany. He was very good-looking and remarkably successful with women.

Soon the Baroness von Berg became his mistress. She had a relative, Renata von Natzmer, who worked in the German War Office. So Sosnowski was able to report that he had begun to establish his spy-ring. Soon information began to flow back to Warsaw, especially as more women who held posts in Government offices were enlisted—among them Fräulein von Jena.

The spy-ring was very expensive, but it was producing a flow of useful information. The approaching rise of Hitler had increased Polish apprehension, and Sosnowski's very large expense accounts were paid.

Then in 1934, when Fräulein von Natzmer's mother came to Berlin, she was surprised at her daughter's prosperity. The girl explained that a German general, a friend of her father, had found her a much better job. Some months later the mother met the general at a party, and naturally thanked him for his kindness to her daughter. But he knew that he had done no such kindness: inquiries began, with the inevitable result.

Sosnowski was sentenced to a long period of imprisonment—but was later exchanged for some German spies captured by the Poles. Fräulein von Jena received a sentence of fifteen years' imprisonment, and von Berg and von Natzmer were condemned to death. They were duly beheaded.

This was the story released by the Nazi Press to the world. The beginning and the end were true—Sosnowski *did* go to Berlin as a spy, and the two women *were* executed in macabre fashion. The rest of the story was fictitious.

When Sosnowski first arrived in Berlin he found that espionage was not quite as easy as he had expected. But on a racecourse he met a German named Rudloff, who worked in the War Office. He was short of money—and became the Pole's first agent. Later von Berg and von Natzmer followed. Sosnowski was delighted.

But the Germans, who had, of course, known that he was a Polish officer, were suspicious of his wealthy way of life, and soon realized the truth. And Sosnowski discovered that his three assistants were all German agents!

They had been deliberately placed in his path, had joined his spy-ring, and had 'inspired' him with information supplied by the German Intelligence staff.

Picture Sosnowski's dilemma. He would be arrested, tried, and sentenced; he would be in disgrace in his own country; and he would for ever lose the luxurious standard of life to which he had become accustomed—whereas the Germans as well as his own people were now prepared to pay him. He was of low moral stature, and decided to carry on. Thereafter he worked under instruction as a *German spy*.

The Poles gradually developed misgivings. Some of Sosnowski's information had proved to be misleading; he had consistently refused to return to Warsaw for consultation; and his spy-ring, continually enlarged, was now *very* expensive.

Then a Polish spy, Gryf-Czajkowski, returned from Germany. He was known to have been 'inspired' by the Germans, and in his interrogation he revealed that Sosnowski was in German pay!

Again the latter was ordered home, but again he made excuses. Then the Germans struck. They knew all about Gryf-Czajkowski: obviously he had denounced Sosnowski, who could still be useful to the Nazis.

Von Berg and von Natzmer were executed. Yet they were *German* agents! The explanation is simple. They belonged to aristocratic families, and Hitler wished to humiliate their class.

Further, the execution would support the new Nazi plan. At the trial the Nazis had treated Sosnowski as a gallant and patriotic spy, never revealing that he had been in their pocket for eight years. Now they schemed to get him appointed as head of the German section of the Polish Secret Service, where he could give them immense assistance. Hence the ease of his exchange for some German spies captured by the Poles. And it was believed that the execution of the two women would help to convince the Poles that Sosnowski had been loyal to them.

This plot failed. On his exchange Sosnowski faced a long and complicated trial in Warsaw, and was again sentenced to fifteen years' imprisonment.

And Fräulein von Jena? She indeed comes under my heading of "Spies who never were"—for she never existed! Sosnowski invented her—and other women on his payroll— solely in order to increase his financial allowances![1]

V

I had to think hard over the inclusion or otherwise in this book of Major André. The Americans hanged him as a spy—but the British buried him in Westminster Abbey!

One of Washington's generals was Benedict Arnold. Though very capable, early in the War of Independence he had been passed over for promotion, and was grievously hurt. When at last he was appointed to command at West Point he had already determined to betray this important supply depot to the British.

[1] For a full account of this fantastic case see *The Sosnowski Affair*, by Bernard Newman.

Major John André, of Swiss extraction, educated at St Paul's School, was sent by the British to negotiate with Arnold. The latter supplied him with plans of West Point, and arranged its surrender after a pseudo-attack. But now André ran into difficulties. A British sloop, the *Vulture*, was to have picked him up, but had been driven off by the fire of an American shore battery. So André had to make his way back to the British lines overland—with Arnold's incriminating papers hidden in his boots!

Then he made a fatal error. He had been sent to Arnold as an envoy, not as a spy—and was in uniform. Now he disobeyed his orders and donned civilian clothes.

Arnold provided him with a guide, who conducted him to a spot almost within sight of the British lines. But almost as soon as he was alone André was held up by three American militiamen. True, he carried a pass from General Arnold— in the name of John Anderson—but he aroused suspicion by attempting to bribe his captors. However, the local unit decided to send him to West Point. André was happy— Arnold would soon arrange his release.

But the tiny yet capable American counter-spy service had been active. British officers had been billeted in a house in Oyster Bay. One evening a guest arrived for dinner—and pocketed a letter awaiting collection by "John Anderson". A girl in the house reported this to her brother—who was one of Washington's Intelligence officers.

Arnold had written to a Captain Tallmadge commending a man named John Anderson, who might pass his way. And now Anderson was revealed as a British officer! He was stopped before reaching West Point—but Arnold escaped.

André was tried by court-martial, and sentenced to be hanged as a spy. The British Commander protested; André was an official envoy who happened to have laid his uniform aside; but legally the Americans were justified. Had André been in uniform he would merely have been held as a prisoner of war. The fact that he put on civilian clothes placed him in the category of a spy. It is rather absurd: he never did any spying, and his clothes were the only evidence against him.

So Major André was hanged. The British Army went into mourning for him, and George III ordered a memorial to his honour in Westminster Abbey. At the end of the war his body was exhumed and buried with full military honours in the Abbey. The bas-relief shows Washington receiving André's petition—not for mercy, but for a soldier's death instead of a degrading hanging. This was refused; but an American wreath of autumn leaves long decorated the Abbey memorial.

VI

These are borderline cases. We can now proceed to examine examples which are clear-cut: their subjects were alleged to be spies, but were not. They do not keep to any set pattern, and each chapter is very different from its neighbour. My records should at least put a damper on the popular habit of dubbing as spies thousands of people who do not deserve the label.

A popular television feature went so far as to class Sir Roger Casement as a spy! The indignation of patriotic Irishmen can be imagined.

TWO

The Dreyfus Case

I

ESPIONAGE IN THE LATTER PART of the nineteenth century was a crude affair, devoid of radio and concealed microphones. Its accustomed methods were almost stereotyped. One was euphemistically called 'the usual channels'. This conventional phrase covered such methods as bribing an employee of a foreign embassy to retrieve the contents of wastepaper-baskets and hand them over to the local service.

The spies were recruited mainly from the petty-criminal classes. They were usually completely unreliable, and might work for both sides. Indeed, a Frenchman recruited by the Germans might report to the French War Office, who would thereafter 'inspire' him with the information he was to pass over. The deliberate forging or falsification of official reports was a recognized method used by most of the spy organizations: it is not remarkable that their achievements were negligible or even misleading. And in most countries the security system was all but a farce.

Almost unique among European espionage systems of the late nineteenth century was that of the British. And it may seem paradoxical to state that its success and the reliability of its information were due to the fact that it was not a 'system' at all! Britain did not use the thousands of plodding, unimaginative, paid-by-the-hour watchers of the Ochrana, nor the mercenary and unreliable, paid-by-results agents of other Continental Intelligence services: she relied largely on the free-lance work of Service officers on leave who liked to combine business with pleasure in the course of a Continental holiday. These men were untrained as spies, and they seldom possessed brilliant brains: but, with little official help and practically no official money to spend, they often achieved remarkable results. Whatever their intellectual shortcomings, these were intensely patriotic men of the highest integrity, and the reports they submitted could be implicitly trusted as accurate.

A random example is that of young Robert Baden-Powell, who during his annual leave went to Austria and posed as an entomologist, sitting on high hills and sketching butterflies, into the drawings of whose wings he incorporated details of Austrian fortifications; and who later gained entry into the closely guarded Kiel naval dockyard and, having noted its secrets, splashed whisky round his collar and tie, staggered a little, and was helped out through the guarded gates by a sympathetic German sentry who wished he had been at such a nice party himself! It is in Intelligence work that the British talent for improvisation shows up at its best.

In France the counter-espionage organization was 'disguised' as the Statistical Section, a ruse which fooled no one, least of all the German spies. It was small—six officers and two clerks.

One of its senior officers was Major Hubert-Joseph Henry, a regular career soldier who had risen from the ranks. He distinguished himself in several colonial wars; his courage was undoubted, but his lack of education was a handicap to his work on 'Statistics'—mainly the faking of information intended for the edification of potential opponents, and the reconstruction of documents from the scraps found in wastepaper-baskets.

It was while engaged on such tasks that he had a shock. One of his agents was a woman named Bastian, who, working in the German Embassy as a housemaid, was well placed to recover the contents of wastepaper-baskets. But on this occasion she had done better. In the hall of the Embassy was a pigeonhole rack in which incoming letters were placed. Seeing one addressed to Colonel von Schwarzkoppen, the German Military Attaché, she had promptly filched it.

The letter was in French, but unsigned. It was evidently a summary of the other and more bulky documents that it enumerated. These included notes on modern artillery developments, protective tactics, and the Madagascar expedition. Henry studied it in alarm. This was obviously written by a French officer, probably a specialist in gunnery; and, on the face of it, this was not the first communication of its kind. Here was no affair of a wastrel spy passing on gossip or doctored information: the French had a traitor in their midst.

This letter became one of the most famous documents in French history: it became known as the *bordereau*, the list.

Who had written it? No one in the Statistical Section recognized the handwriting. But surely a regimental officer could not cover so wide a range of information—the traitor must be an officer on the Staff. And the list included items concerned with several sections of the Staff. The only officers who made the rounds of all the sections were the Staff 'learners', newcomers to the work. Obviously, it was agreed, this was where the search must begin. Thence progress was rapid, for one of the Staff 'learners' was Jewish.

II

Captain Alfred Dreyfus came of a respected Alsatian family—a wealthy Jewish family, so that he did not need the financial rewards of espionage. The family was passionately French in its loyalty, and after the German victory of 1871—when Germany annexed Alsace and part of Lorraine from defeated France—had opted for French nationality.

Alfred was a man of high intelligence and ability. He was not liked, for he was apt to criticize his superiors—which does not make for popularity. He was vain and boastful. But his ability was so outstanding that he could not be denied a position on the Staff—the first Jewish officer to achieve such a distinction.

A generation earlier France had housed no more than 80,000 Jews. After the murder of the Tsar Alexander II in 1881, when pogroms became a favourite sport in Russia, thousands of Jews fled to the West—120,000 to France. They were not over-welcome: few knew any language other than Russian and Yiddish. Anti-Semitism, at first a feeble growth, rapidly gathered strength—above all in the French officer corps, which was strongly Catholic and blatantly reactionary.

So, when the process of elimination appeared to narrow the choice of the traitor to the five Staff probationer officers, Dreyfus was the obvious suspect. There was no real investigation: it was simply assumed that he was guilty. Thus, before he was charged—before he had any suspicion as to

what was happening—he was inveigled into copying a couple
of lines from a letter: actually from the *bordereau*. Later the
officer in charge of the test gave evidence that Dreyfus's
hand trembled—but he did not mention that it was a very
cold day and that Dreyfus's fingers were numbed.

And when Dreyfus was formally charged the responsible
officer ostentatiously displayed a revolver.

"I am innocent. Kill me if you wish," Dreyfus
shouted.

"It is not our business to do the executioner's work. It is
yours."

But Dreyfus refused to take the hint. Protesting his innocence, he handed over his keys and requested a search of
his apartment. It revealed nothing.

A leading handwriting expert was called in. To the dismay
of the Staff, he declared emphatically that Dreyfus was not
the writer of the *bordereau*. Next the Staff turned to the
famous Alphonse Bertillon, whose system of anthropometric
measurement for the identification of criminals had had
great effects on police work. But Bertillon had no qualifications as a handwriting expert. Further, his opinion was
influenced when he was informed that there were other proofs
that Dreyfus had written the *bordereau*. So he came to the
amazing conclusion that Dreyfus had forged an imitation of
his own handwriting! And this opinion was admitted as
'evidence'.

This was typical of the course of the trial. Searches of
Dreyfus's rooms had revealed nothing. Therefore he "had
made away with everything". The *opinions* of Staff officers
were accepted as evidence, and hearsay was admitted. Finally, after the court had retired to consider its verdict, eight
documents were submitted to it. None had the slightest

connection with Dreyfus, but a covering letter made them appear to incriminate him. The submission was quite illegal, for the documents were not shown to the defence counsel, who could have demolished their 'evidence'.

Dreyfus was found guilty and sentenced to life imprisonment. First he was degraded: on a formal parade his insignia were ripped from his uniform, and his sword was broken. Still protesting his innocence, he was shipped to Devil's Island, off French Guiana. There his sufferings were appalling. Only a strong man could have survived—a man determined to redeem his honour.

III

Dreyfus had protested his innocence: his brother Mathieu was prepared to spend the family fortune in proving it. Yet he had nothing but his brother's word to go on—the 'evidence' in the trial was apparently a State secret.

So far the Dreyfus case had been little known and attracted little attention outside Army circles. Dreyfus might have languished to his death on Devil's Island, but for another incident in the secret war—via the 'usual channels' of the German Embassy wastepaper-basket.

The invaluable housemaid had conveyed its contents to the Statistical Section. There an officer found a *petit bleu* ripped into more than fifty pieces—a *petit bleu* was an express letter used in the Paris district, not unlike our air-mail letters, but of a deeper blue. With great patience the officer pieced the fragments together. He recognized the code signature of the sender, who was evidently dissatisfied with his letter, and had torn it up. The sender was Colonel von Schwarzkoppen, the German Military Attaché.

His note read: "Before all I await a more detailed explanation on the matter in question. Will you, therefore, be good enough to let me have it in writing to enable me to decide whether I can continue my relations with the firm of R. or not."

To an Intelligence officer the meaning was plain: someone had offered Schwarzkoppen documents or plans, and the German wanted fuller details. The officer put the reconstructed *petit bleu* before his chief.

"This is frightening," he said.

"*Mon Dieu!*" cried the latter. "Another Dreyfus case!"

Lieutenant-Colonel Marie-Georges Picquart was, like Dreyfus, an Alsatian. He was the youngest officer of his rank in the French Army, and was believed to have a brilliant future before him. He was appointed chief of the Statistical Section over the head of Major Henry, who had been so intimately concerned with the *bordereau* which had led to Dreyfus's trial—which Picquart had attended in an official capacity.

It was natural that he should suspect that the *petit bleu* had revealed another Dreyfus. But further thought prompted another idea—might it not suggest that Dreyfus was innocent? But when he mentioned this possibility to his seniors he was warned against doing anything which could upset the verdict of the court-martial.

Picquart was not only clever but honest. He persisted— and his seniors resorted to a plan made famous by David. He was posted to the army in Tunis, and his general was ordered to "assign him to a post of danger".

Before leaving the Statistical Section, however, he had followed up the clue of the *petit bleu*. It was addressed to a Major Esterhazy.

This officer was descended from an illegitimate branch of a famous Hungarian family, but in blood and upbringing he was French. He was a poor soldier and a dissolute gambler, constantly hard up, and almost devoid of morals. He was of the stuff of traitors, just as Dreyfus was not.

After the incident of the *petit bleu* he was watched, and seen to visit the German Embassy. Further, Picquart obtained two letters in Esterhazy's handwriting. It was identical with that of the *bordereau*. The reaction of the Army chiefs to Picquart has been pointed out. But while the latter was on service in Tunis further developments occurred. The Paris *Éclair* discovered that documents not available to the defence had influenced the court—a violation of the law—and *Le Matin* managed to get a photograph of the *bordereau*, which it published.

Mathieu Dreyfus seized on this disclosure and publicized it. The French are keen and ardent investigators. It did not take long for amateur detectives to prove that the handwriting of the *bordereau* was not that of Dreyfus, but *was* that of Esterhazy. Senior politicians began to press for the case to be reopened.[1]

But the Army was not yet defeated or even discouraged. Major Esterhazy was tried by court-martial—and acquitted! What was more, Colonel Picquart was accused of having released official documents—to the friends of Dreyfus, presumably—and was himself tried and found guilty.

But by this time Paris was buzzing with excitement. It

[1] Much later it was revealed that, when Esterhazy first offered his services to Colonel von Schwarzkoppen, the German Attaché had refused them. He was accustomed to deal with the *canaille* class of spy, and could not believe that a French senior officer could act as a traitor. Only on a direct order from Berlin did he open negotiations.

was not a case of mass passions—the ordinary people were
interested but not aroused. It was in the main a battle between
a conservative coalition of the Army, aided by the clerical
organizations, and the liberals of the professional classes.

The latter gained an outstanding recruit—the novelist
Émile Zola. He wrote his famous letter *J'accuse*, and it was
published by a newspaper editor of immense courage—
Georges Clemenceau, later "the Tiger" of France.

It had a tremendous impact. The first reaction was un-
foreseen—the right-wing factions of the Press and politics
aroused anti-Jewish riots in dozens of cities. There were
open fights in the French parliament, and intellectuals who
demanded a retrial of Dreyfus walked in peril of their lives.

Zola was not the man to suffer violent opposition without
reply. He was arrested, and prosecuted, and sentenced, but
on appeal his conviction was quashed. After all, he had
merely demanded justice for a man who assuredly had not
received it.

The Dreyfus case aroused a dozen passions. The first was,
of course, anti-Semitism. One Deputy screamed of an opponent: "He has dared to say, 'I do not know if Dreyfus
is guilty or not.' This is stupid, because all Jews are traitors."
Hitler could scarcely have bettered such an outburst.

Then the quarrel widened: the common man was led in
one way by the intellectuals, and in the other by the reactionaries of politics, Church, and Army. The first faction had the
passion, the second the power. Zola was again brought
to trial, and defended himself and his cause vigorously. But
maybe his actions were more influential than his words.
Believing that justice had vanished from the French scene,
he fled to England.

The impact of this was tremendous. It particularly affected

one man of only modest intelligence—Major Henry. He professed his belief that Dreyfus had been rightly convicted: he held that it would be disastrous to France if the Establishment were to be proved in the wrong. Even in the trial of Dreyfus he had perjured himself. He gave evidence that a "man of honour" had told him that Dreyfus was a traitor. It was amazing that such hearsay should be admitted: it was even more remarkable that a senior officer of counter-espionage should lie. Henry believed that someone *must* be condemned for the crime: it was of no concern to him whether the man was Dreyfus or another.

And now, with the pro-Dreyfus party obviously gaining ground, Henry—now chief of the Statistical Section—made his final throw—a fantastic piece of folly. He forged a document which purported to show that Dreyfus had spied for both Germany and Italy; it also implicated Picquart—who had been expelled from the French Army and imprisoned for his courage in supporting Dreyfus.

Unfortunately for him, Henry was an incompetent plotter, and his palpable forgery was revealed as such. Hopelessly cornered, he confessed—and killed himself.

Some people believe that Henry himself was a traitor. This is improbable. His outstanding fault was stupidity.

The news of Henry's suicide startled the culprit, Esterhazy—who advertised his guilt by prompt flight to England. Now the way was at last clear for the march of justice.

Yet reactionaries are notoriously slow to see the obvious. Dreyfus was brought back from Devil's Island. The supreme Cour de Cassation quashed his conviction, and announced that Esterhazy was the author of the *bordereau*. It then handed Dreyfus over to an Army court-martial so that it might "rectify its mistake".

c

But in this fantastic case nothing went according to expectations. The Dreyfus faction were already celebrating their victory when the Army produced more forged documents, purporting to be letters from Dreyfus to the Kaiser Wilhelm II, annotated in the Kaiser's own hand. On the basis of this fantastic invention, Dreyfus was found guilty and sentenced to ten years' imprisonment! The poor man must have thought that the Fates were against him.[1]

He was promptly pardoned by the President of the Republic—who was advised that the case had aroused such fury that civil war or revolution might be expected should the conviction stand. Dreyfus accepted the pardon, on condition that he might work to prove his innocence. Even with the Establishment hopelessly discredited, this took time. Not until 1906, eleven years after his first conviction, was his honour restored. He returned to the Army, retired, and returned again at the outbreak of war in 1914. Then he was promoted to brigadier-general, and served his country manfully. He died in 1935, quiet and honourable to the last.

The other characters in the long-drawn-out drama are also dead. Picquart was restored to the Army with honour when the truth about Dreyfus was admitted. He became a general, and when Clemenceau formed his first Cabinet in 1906 he made Picquart Minister of War. When Clemenceau fell, in the inevitable turmoil of French politics, Picquart returned

---

[1] Dreyfus did not impress even unbiased witnesses at his trial. But he was a sick man, racked with fever. One of his tortures had been that of silence—his guards had been forbidden to exchange a word with him. For years the deathly silence was maintained. Dreyfus had almost forgotten how to talk—and had certainly lost part of his vocabulary. Small wonder that he sounded confused and hesitant when giving evidence. And his confusion must have been heightened by the farrago of nonsense placed before the court.

to the Army. In 1914, however, he was thrown from his horse, and died from his injuries.

Émile Zola died in 1902, before Dreyfus was officially exonerated, but the French Government made belated amends by transferring his remains to the Panthéon in Paris; and, as if to illustrate the deep cleavage of French opinion, a fanatic attempted to assassinate Dreyfus during the burial ceremony!

Esterhazy was careful not to leave England—he had been condemned in France in his absence. For a time he lived with and on a woman who kept a brothel, and when she turned him out he existed by various unsavoury adventures. At last he retired to Harpenden, where he died in 1923.

Colonel von Schwarzkoppen commanded a German division during the First World War, but in 1917 he was taken ill and moved to Berlin. On his deathbed he suddenly awoke from a coma to shout, "Frenchmen, listen to me! Dreyfus is innocent! It was all just intrigue and forgery!"

He might have said that earlier: but, of course, he would not have been believed, for it is everywhere traditional to deny the employment of spies.

Technically there were no spies in the Dreyfus case. There was a traitor, Esterhazy, and a stupid and deluded patriot, Henry. The only spy involved was the maid who stole the contents of the German Embassy wastepaper-baskets!

Certainly the character who emerges from the affair with the greatest honour was the Jewish officer Alfred Dreyfus.

IV

In this chapter I have merely outlined the principal events in this extraordinary affair. To do it fuller justice I should have related them to the turbulent course of French politics—but this would have demanded an entire book to itself. In all, the case dragged on from December 1893 to October 1906. In that time France had six presidents and twelve prime ministers! (This was not out of the ordinary: during the last eighty years France has had 127 Cabinets.)

French political instability was one of the features which continuously intruded into the case. Another is difficult for our generation to understand, accustomed as we are to a strong French Republic. In the eighteen-nineties the Republic was but a feeble infant, with countless enemies, ranging from left-wing groups which wanted a different sort of Republic to Royalists who wanted no Republic of any kind. Dreyfus's second conviction, had it been allowed to stand, might well have led to a revolt by his supporters; once that had begun, all other factions would have joined in, for or against; in the resultant confusion the original complaint would have been forgotten.

Yet another dominating feature was the possibility of war with Germany, for which France was actively preparing. Had Dreyfus been arraigned as a British or a Spanish spy the case would never have aroused so great a furore.

With the possible exception of Henry, the officers concerned in the first action against Dreyfus acted in good faith. Their fault was that they believed what they wanted to believe. The affair erupted at a nervous moment—when the defence schemes against Germany were being replanned and the famous 75-mm. field gun had just been produced. A traitor at such a time would have been a disaster. There was no conspiracy: the senior officers did believe in Dreyfus's guilt; they were so nervous of the potential consequences of treachery that they could not view the evidence realistically.

At first anti-Semitism was deliberately suppressed in public reports of the affair; it increased later as passions became more violent. The trial of Zola was a turning-point in the case, involving the French intelligentsia and students and bringing it right out into the open.

Then the politicians came on the scene. They knew little about the case, but rapidly took sides, some only to change them quickly on Henry's suicide. It was they who fostered the idea that the case was a conspiracy of the Army and the Church against the common people; they would have been more effective had they been sincere. Propaganda became a powerful weapon—unscrupulous as ever.

The results of the affair were important. The Army Command had to submit to reforms—highly necessary in view of the impending war with Germany. The quarrel between Church and State, which had begun with the foundation of the Republic, now became fierce and unbridled. Confidence in French justice was weakened.

A flood of passions and prejudices inundated France for a generation ahead. In fact, the Dreyfus case almost certainly influenced the onset of the First World War: the German leaders believed that France was so weakened and demoralized by the affair that she would prove an easy prey. They were very nearly right.

THREE

Spy in Parliament?

I

NO WRITER OF SENSATIONAL SECRET SERVICE fiction
would dare to invent such a character as Trebitsch Lincoln.
Readers would feel that their credulity was being strained
far beyond its limits.

Lincoln was a Hungarian with some talent as a writer, an
effective orator, an industrious research worker, a man of
considerable political acumen, a cunning and unscrupulous
wriggler out of awkward situations—a born politician, in
fact. He was also a pathological liar, a sneak-thief, swindler,
forger, and theological contortionist.

His character was complex; his career can only be described as incredible. Converted from Judaism, he became an
Irish Presbyterian missionary and later Anglican curate of
a Kentish parish; a Member of Parliament; nearly an oilfield
millionaire; a war-time censor; a self-confessed German spy;
a high official in a German monarchist Government; political and military adviser to several Chinese war-lords; a
Buddhist abbot; probably a Japanese secret agent.

The very few people today who remember one of the most

38

extraordinary men of the century would almost unanimously recall him only as a German spy working against Britain. That was the only detail of his story which has no single fact in favour of it and all the probabilities against it.

This colourful character was born in April 1879 in the little Hungarian market town of Paks, on the banks of the Danube, about sixty miles south of Budapest. His original name was Ignatz Trebitsch. His strictly orthodox Jewish father was a prosperous partner in a firm which owned a fleet of barges trading up and down the Danube.

Business losses in 1895 forced Trebitsch senior to interrupt his children's education. But Ignatz did not find himself a steady job as did his elder brother. Instead he took to haunting the cafés of Budapest, telling extravagant stories of romantic foreign cities which he had never visited and world-famous men whom he had never met. It was a welcome surprise to find that local newspapers were prepared to pay money for these fictions and publish them as facts.

The ambitious and unscrupulous teenager decided that it would be pleasant and instructive to visit the places he had pictured so vividly in his imagination, and he solved the problem of expenses by stealing and selling the gold watch of one of his married sisters. With the proceeds he made his first trip abroad, to Hamburg, Paris, London, and Bristol.

From England, Ignatz returned briefly to Hungary, but did not stay long. In 1898 he turned up again in Hamburg, where the destitute youth seems to have found it possible to obtain free board and lodging as a prospective convert at the local Irish Presbyterian Mission to the Jews. He 'worked his passage' by becoming an Irish Presbyterian, and was baptized in the rather un-Celtic name of Ignatius Timotheus Trebitsch on Christmas Day in that year.

He was upset when the very practical Irish Presbyterians then turned him out of his room, as it had served its purpose and was needed for another prospective convert. The object of the Mission was, after all, to convert Jews and not to offer unlimited free board and lodging to baptized Presbyterians. The easiest way of continuing to live without paying his way seemed to be to study for the ministry. So Ignatz entered an Irish Presbyterian seminary in Schleswig-Holstein, where he combined business with pleasure by courting a gawky pregnant Lutheran girl named Margarethe Kahlor—a courtship which the rector of the seminary pointed out was against the rules for theological students.

Even at the risk of jeopardizing his career, however, Ignatz refused to give up his Gretchen, as he called her, and after a few uneasy months he accepted the offer of a free passage to Canada as prospective assistant to the Mission's pastor in Montreal. Some little time elapsed before his appointment took effect and his salary became payable. He spent this difficult period in a few poorly paid odd jobs and in studying English, his meagre earnings being augmented by money sent from Germany by his faithful Gretchen.

He had a definite talent for oratory, and seems to have had some success in his missionary efforts. In his spare time the studies interrupted in Germany were completed at McGill University. At last he qualified and became free to take a wife. He sent for Gretchen, and they were married in Montreal in July 1901. Her baby Julius, whom she had been carrying when she first met Ignatz, was left in Germany.

Early in the following year the ambitious Ignatz had another difference of opinion with his superiors, this time on the question of delayed promotion. At about the same time he was approached by a Canadian official of the London Mission to the Jews. Ignatz readily changed his brand of religion almost overnight, and after a few more months of study was ordained an Anglican deacon at the end of the year. And in that theologically free-and-easy home it does not seem to have worried him that Gretchen's second baby, which died in infancy, was baptized a Lutheran.

His work again seems to have been successful, but again he fell out with his superiors, this time because they would not advance him a few dollars of his stipend, and in mid-1903 he took Gretchen back to Germany.

With his knack of contacting and convincing influential people, Ignatz would today have been an outstanding success in the modern profession of public-relations officer. Only a few months after his return to Germany we find him in Lambeth Palace, exerting his undoubted powers of persuasion on no less a person than the Archbishop of Canterbury. And in February 1904 the Jewish Hungarian and former Irish Presbyterian became Anglican curate of the little parish of Appledore, in Kent.

The Reverend Ignatz Trebitsch, his German Lutheran wife, and somebody else's son Julius—now legitimatized by adoption—were very unhappy at Appledore. His impassioned sermons, delivered in a pronounced East European accent, baffled the village shopkeepers and farmworkers who made up his congregation. Gretchen's almost complete ignorance of the English language kept her indoors while her husband did the shopping.

It may be difficult for present-day readers to picture the early Edwardian attitude towards foreigners. British working people, particularly in country districts, regarded them as

either evil or contemptible. At about the time when Ignatz
was preaching to the Kentish villagers a Pole named Severin
Antoniovitch Klosowski, who called himself "George
Chapman", was tried for murder at the Old Bailey. And his
own Counsel said casually of the cowering prisoner in the
dock, "This man is a hated alien, with all that that implies."

Gretchen was sorry when she heard of the death of her
father, but Ignatz was delighted when he heard that she had
been left a small legacy. He at once decided that the Church
of England offered insufficient scope for a man with his
talents and ambitions. The immortal souls of Appledore
could now save themselves from hell as far as he was concerned. He decided to become a businessman.

Living on Gretchen's small capital, he took a house at
Hampton, in Middlesex, where his mother-in-law joined
them. And the rather handsome new 'City gent', with his
upcurled moustache, dark, wavy, centre-parted hair, and
gold-rimmed *pince-nez*, began to commute between Hampton
and the City.

During this period he soon found that the name of Ignatius Timotheus Trebitsch made a poor impression on the
jingoistic Edwardian financiers with whom he was trying so
hard to do business. He was always something of a hero-
worshipper, and there is for once no reason to disbelieve his
statement that he adopted a new surname because of his
admiration for Abraham Lincoln. He changed his name by
deed-poll to "Ignatius Timothy Trebitsch Lincoln", but
when he later became notorious, journalists did not trouble
to check with Somerset House, and he was seldom referred
to thereafter as other than "Trebitsch Lincoln".

In various odd jobs on the fringe of the advertising world
Ignatz was, rather surprisingly, not a success. Perhaps as a

house-to-house canvasser he found that doorstep oratory offered insufficient scope for his talents. He needed a bigger audience than a single housewife. He had found it easier to sell an intangible, such as religion, than to sell domestic gadgets. So he started to sell another intangible—temperance—and his lectures were immediately successful. Through Quaker contacts in his new milieu he was able to meet and impress so shrewd a character as the Quaker sociologist Seebohm Rowntree. It was the beginning of an association that was to have long-term effects on Lincoln's career.

Dazzled by Lincoln's flamboyant self-confidence, Rowntree engaged him to carry out a programme of sociological research on the Continent. This suited Lincoln very well, as he had a good salary, liberal expenses, and introductions to prominent men. In return he served his employer conscientiously, travelling widely, conducting numerous interviews, and tabulating a great deal of useful economic information over a period of several years. But ambition soon drove him on to greater heights.

By 1909, when he was only thirty, Lincoln appeared to be on the threshold of a career which would have seemed a fantastic improbability less than ten years previously. The former destitute Hungarian sneak-thief, the former Irish Presbyterian missionary, the former frustrated Anglican village curate, the former down-at-heel, door-to-door salesman, had become a naturalized British subject, an apparently prosperous English gentleman, an expert on economics, a member of the highly respectable National Liberal Club, and Parliamentary candidate in the constituency of Darlington, where his large house accommodated his wife, two sons, mother-in-law, and secretary. That was in August 1909. It had been quick work.

II

It is an interesting coincidence that during the weeks when
Lincoln was nursing the constituency he was so soon to
represent in Parliament, the British Government had become
so worried by the German-spy menace that on August 23rd,
1909, a new department known as the Special Intelligence
Bureau was set up in a small room of the War Office in
Whitehall. It had an initial staff of one regular Army officer,
a certain Captain Kell of the South Staffordshire Regiment,
who—after a thirty-one-year career as one of the world's
greatest but least known spy-catchers—was to retire in 1940
as Major-General Sir Vernon Kell, K.B.E., C.B., Director
of the department which has become world-famous as MI5.
It is tempting, if unprofitable, to speculate as to the date
when—as in due course happened—young Captain Kell added
to his card index an entry for the Hungarian of dubious
antecedents who was making political history in Darlington.

For many years Darlington had been represented in
Parliament by members of the Pike-Pease family. It had
long been regarded as a safe seat for the Unionists, that almost
forgotten label for what is now the Conservative Party. It
seemed incredible then—it seems incredible now—that a
member of a well-known and well-respected local family
should have had anything to fear from the competition of
a recently arrived Hungarian, who had been the subject
of a foreign country until some eight months before the
election.

But the facts are on record. On January 15th, 1910, over
95 per cent of the Darlington electorate registered their votes,
and that staunch English Liberal Ignatius Timothy Trebitsch
Lincoln was elected, after a recount, by a majority of 29

votes. From time to time throughout Lincoln's career there was the narrowest possible margin between victory and defeat. This time he was lucky. And one can picture young Captain Kell in his Whitehall cubicle adding a note to his index card for "I. T. T. Lincoln, M.P."

It was unfortunate for the new Member for Darlington that at that vital milestone in his career—in days before M.P.s were paid—he was very short of money. His plans to improve the lot of the British people had to be temporarily shelved while he dealt with the more immediate problem of improving the lot of his wife and family. And—let us give credit where it is all too seldom due—his plans were so shrewd and far-seeing that in the end he was within a few days of becoming a wealthy man. He decided to deal in oil, which was then beginning to replace coal as fuel for the navies and merchant ships of the world.

So he borrowed a few pounds for expenses and travelled to newly discovered oilfields in Eastern Europe, and on his way he was lucky enough to meet and recruit an Austrian legal expert on oilfield deals. The lawyer reported that options on a number of small oil companies could be secured for £10,000, which Lincoln obtained from Seebohm Rowntree. Back in London, Lincoln was delighted to find that a financier was prepared to raise a quarter of a million pounds to complete the purchase and amalgamation of the oil companies. This perfectly honest and highly promising speculation might in normal conditions have made Lincoln a wealthy man.

Unfortunately for Lincoln, however, conditions were far from normal, and he had insufficient resources to be able to wait until they improved. So he acted as other speculators since his time have done—he kept creditors at bay by producing a guarantee on which he had forged the signature of Seebohm Rowntree. And if the oilfield deal had begun to produce profits within a reasonable time he would have been able to retrieve and destroy the document without anyone being the wiser. Similar cases on a vaster scale have come to light from time to time—Clarence Hatry and Ivar Kreuger are two random examples—and one cannot help wondering how many other such forgeries of documents used temporarily for credit purposes have never been revealed.

Where Lincoln was particularly unlucky, or particularly shortsighted, was that he committed his crime during the uneasy weeks between the Sarajevo assassination and the outbreak of the First World War. Every financier in Europe was calling in loans and refusing credits. Lincoln had been beaten by time.

So he was adjudged bankrupt, resigned his seat in Parliament, and his only assets were holdings of dubious value in Eastern Europe. It was only later that he learned that shortly before war was declared oil had begun to spurt from the Rumanian drillings and flow into the Galician pipelines. But by then he had had to sell his holdings for a song.

When war broke out Lincoln applied for a post as an Intelligence Officer. He was turned down, but accepted a post in the Military Censorship, for which his knowledge of languages qualified him.

III

It is convenient at this point to deal with the ridiculous statements that have been made to the effect that Lincoln had been a German spy before the outbreak of the First World War.

The German General Staff regarded the small British professional army of those days as a negligible factor in any future war. What Germany really feared was the great British Navy, against which all espionage activity in Britain was directed. So of the twenty-two German agents in Britain all were stationed in seaports and naval bases, with the exception of a 'pillar-box' in London, through whom their instructions and reports passed. Which was very convenient for Captain Kell, who intercepted their correspondence and, if necessary, 'doctored' their reports before passing them for delivery to Berlin.

There were two other German spies who had no fixed bases in Britain: Dr Armgaard Karl Graves before the War, and Lieutenant Karl Hans Lody shortly after war broke out. Both were specially trained as observers of naval matters. Both were caught within weeks of arriving in Britain. Graves, sentenced in peace-time, was imprisoned: Lody, sentenced in war-time, was shot. Compared with these men, who, if not very efficient as spies, could recognize the silhouette of every ship in the Royal Navy from miles away, Lincoln as a naval spy would have been just a joke.

And, quite apart from the general question of German Intelligence policy, Lincoln's busy life had been passed between Darlington and Westminster, with occasional trips to Eastern Europe. He would have had no time to make systematic observation of the movements of British warships in and out of their bases. His financial position does not suggest that he was being subsidized by the Wilhelmstrasse, who might have been expected to be fairly generous to a traitor M.P. And, lastly, even the rather incompetent German spy-masters would have hesitated to employ on secret work in Britain this flamboyant, garrulous individual who attracted attention wherever he went, who was obviously of alien origin, and who still spoke English with a foreign accent.

As a postal censor Lincoln lasted only a few weeks, and it is not clear why he resigned. Had he been found to be a spy he would, of course, have been tried and, if found guilty, hanged. It seems likely that he abused his position of trust by smuggling abroad inquiries about his oilfield deals, which was illegal, of course, but did no particular harm to the British war effort. And again the question of finance arises. German spy-masters would have been generous to an agent in the British censorship. So it seems significant that almost immediately after leaving his official post Lincoln was in the hands of moneylenders.

He attempted to extend the duration of a loan overdue for repayment by again forging the signature of Seebohm Rowntree, among others, but this time, after some delay, his crime came to the knowledge of his victims. His arrest and trial for forgery became inevitable, and it was surprising —perhaps not least to Lincoln himself—that weeks elapsed before anything was done.

During the last weeks of freedom he was ever to spend in Britain Lincoln was working on a staggering scheme, which most of his biographers quote as an example of his activities as a spy. The scheme was that he should approach German officials in a neutral country, offer his services as a spy, and reveal the imminent movements of a small force of British warships. This would be accurate information about a decoy force which the Germans would be allowed to intercept and destroy. The exploit would be repeated, with a similar result, after which the delighted Germans could be expected to place implicit faith in the reports of this reliable new agent. Finally he would report a prospective sortie by a much more

powerful British naval force, which would lure forth from
its lair at Kiel the entire German North Sea Fleet. A greatly
superior British fleet would be lying in wait, and German
naval power would be smashed at one blow.

This suggestion certainly reached high levels in Whitehall,
but there is no evidence that it was ever taken very seriously.
Such information as eventually leaked out indicates, in fact,
that Lincoln was already under Secret Service observation
as a suspected spy.

Lincoln had very little time left. He knew that at any
moment he might be arrested for forgery. Without waiting
for official approval of his scheme he went to Rotterdam and
called on the German Consul-General, but the latter does
not seem to have considered whatever Lincoln said to be of
sufficient interest to make a note of. Back in London, Lincoln
had several interviews with Captain (later Admiral) "Blinker"
Hall, Chief of Naval Intelligence, but nothing was done.
The time was mid-January 1915, and—an important point
to bear in mind—Lincoln's passport was due to expire on the
last day of that month.

There has been nearly half a century of speculation as to
Lincoln's real motives in his 'decoy fleet' scheme, mostly
based on the incorrect assumption that he was already a well-
established German spy who, by betraying the scheme to the
Germans, would ensure that it should be the British and not
the German warships that would be destroyed.

Had Lincoln really been a German spy with a record of
reporting reliable information, it is conceivable that German Secret Service officials might have listened with cautious interest to his ideas. But in that case he would, of
course, have communicated with them by previously arranged undercover channels. Any amateur of Intelligence work

D

would have known that the highly efficient British Secret
Service kept a close watch on German representatives in
neutral countries, and on all those—particularly British
subjects—who contacted them. The mere fact that Lincoln
called openly upon the German Consul-General in Rotterdam is sufficient proof that he omitted the most elementary
Intelligence precautions, and that he could not have been
at that date in German pay. And it may be hardly necessary
to stress the fact that he would certainly not have been in
German service without pay, especially at that disastrous
stage of his financial affairs.

So, if it be agreed that there was practically no possibility of
his being at that date a German spy, he could not have
been naïve enough to imagine that the Germans would risk
their precious battleships at the suggestion of a British
subject who had turned up out of the blue asking for employment as a spy and a few hundred marks on account.

There should never have been the slightest doubt as to
Lincoln's motive. It was simply that he was desperate to
raise some money quickly and easily. He knew that it was
only a matter of time before he was arrested for forgery, with
ample proof of his guilt. His only alternative to an inevitable
prison sentence was to escape abroad. He had no money
and very little time, his passport being due so soon to expire.
With no loyalty to either Britain or Germany, he hoped to
collect some cash in advance for his 'decoy fleet' scheme from
Britain or Germany or both. And once he had reached the
temporary sanctuary of a neutral country, what might eventually be decided about his scheme by either of the countries
concerned would have ceased to interest him.

There is close liaison between Britain's Military and Naval
Intelligence Departments, and Captain Kell would have

passed on all that he knew about Lincoln to Captain Hall of the Admiralty. But there was a vital detail missing from his dossier: Was he or was he not a German spy? In such circumstances it is an old and obvious Intelligence routine to 'stall'. A paid spy can afford to wait. An innocent man with no overt source of income cannot. So that Lincoln's state of increasing financial panic was one more indication that he was not a spy, because if he had been he would have found ample funds awaiting him in Rotterdam.

Working to the closest possible time limit, Lincoln dashed up to Liverpool, and just managed to catch a liner sailing for the United States on January 30th. In less than twenty-four hours his passport expired. And at about the same time Scotland Yard detectives visited Gretchen with a warrant to arrest her husband on forgery charges. It was a narrow escape.

IV

In neutral America Lincoln was, for the time being, safe from immediate arrest. He could not be sent back to Britain to face charges of treason or espionage, which are not extraditable crimes. And although he could be extradited for forgery, it was likely to be a lengthy procedure which he would deal with when the necessity arose. A more pressing question was that of how he could live and pay his way.

In those days German paymasters in America were generously subsidizing saboteurs and anti-British propagandists, among the latter of whom the most notorious were such disreputable characters as George Sylvester Viereck and the black magician Aleister Crowley. It would have been a considerable scoop to recruit for propaganda purposes so respectable a character as a British ex-Member of Parliament,

into whose pockets the dollars would have poured as soon as
Berlin had authenticated him as an established agent. But in
New York he remained desperate for money. There is not the
slightest evidence that he ever received a cent from German
secret funds in America, or that he ever even approached
German representatives. Had he done so it is likely that his
name would have appeared in the records of secret payments
made by the notorious German Military Attaché in Washington, Franz von Papen, who had the dangerous habit of record-
ing such incriminating details on his cheque-book stubs. His
records were in due course captured by the British Secret
Service. Lincoln's name was not among them.

How Lincoln tried to raise funds was to write anti-British
articles for sale to certain New York newspapers. This was a
complete waste of time, because Anglophobe editors did not
need to pay for such stuff. It was available free from German
propaganda hand-outs, as Lincoln would have known had he
been a German agent. At the end of what had been a disappointing interview in the offices of the *New York World*
Lincoln made an almost casual reference to his 'decoy fleet'
scheme. This aroused immediate interest: if it came off it
would be sensational news. Never slow to take a hint, Lincoln
went on to invent sensational details of his career as a spy,
without mentioning that the 'decoy fleet' scheme had never
had the slightest chance of being put into effect—had in fact
existed only in his vivid imagination.

So a relieved and delighted Lincoln bounced out of the
newspaper office restored to his usual mood of flamboyant
optimism, assured that the story of his adventures as a
German spy would earn him a small fortune. And he did not
bother about the trivial detail that he had never been a
spy for Germany or any other country, and had no know-

ledge whatever of the techniques of espionage. The technique
with which he was completely familiar was that of sensational
journalism. Like so many of the feature writers commissioned to produce 'expert' articles on a subject of which
they are completely ignorant, Lincoln headed straight for
the nearest public library.

For days he studied all the memoirs of genuine spies that
he could find, newspaper accounts of recent espionage trials,
and a certain amount of scissors-and-paste stuff which gave
him a fourth-form schoolboy's knowledge of codes and
secret inks—material which, as every student of Intelligence
work knows, must necessarily be out of date before it is
allowed to be published.

Then he shut himself up in his cheap rented room in Brooklyn, wrote a flattering account of his own career, and worked
in nudge-and-wink, 'now-it-can-be-told' paragraphs based
on the public-library researches, for which his years of work
with Seebohm Rowntree had trained him.

On June 13th, 1915, the *New York World* published
'Revelations of I. T. T. Lincoln, Former Member of Parliament, Who Became a German Spy!" This nonsense was
reprinted in *The Times* of London, indignant questions were
asked in Parliament, and the ridiculous legend of master-spy
Trebitsch Lincoln was launched upon a credulous world.
I hope I have already shown that, as far as his confessions of
espionage went, they did not contain a word of truth.

V

At this point the purpose of our present study has been
served; the legend of Lincoln the German spy has, I trust,
been destroyed for ever; and he might well be left to rot in the

Shanghai grave in which the Venerable Buddhist Abbot
Chao Kung was buried twenty years ago. But to readers who
have perhaps never heard of Lincoln it may be of interest if
I summarize as briefly as possible the remainder of the
kaleidoscopic career of this extraordinary man.

Lincoln was that fortunately rather rare type of man who,
according to prison reformers and optimistic sentimentalists,
does not exist—a type who is constitutionally incapable of
acting in an honest way if a dishonest way can possibly be
devised, a type who is incapable of repentance and reform,
but a type of whom I have personally known several examples. This incurable inclination towards the crooked path
has no relation whatsoever to talents. Some such men become petty criminals and spend most of their unhappy lives
in prison. Others are more clever and make vast fortunes,
such as some of the American financiers of the mid-nine-
teenth century. Others are unlucky, such as those contrasting
characters Ivar Kreuger and Horatio Bottomley. And we
can properly class Lincoln among the definitely unlucky ones,
because if his oil-wells had begun to gush a mere few days
earlier than they actually did he might well have become a
millionaire and a powerful and respected member of the
Liberal Party.

The dollars that Lincoln received for his sensational lies
in the New York newspapers soon ran out, and, as he was
never very anxious to pay his way by doing an honest job
of work, he decided that the quickest and easiest way of
earning a few more dishonest dollars would be to expand his
articles into a book. He was working on this effort when he
was arrested and held for extradition to England on forgery
charges.

Nearly ten months elapsed between Lincoln's arrest early

in August 1915 and the date when he sailed for England in the custody of a Scotland Yard officer at the end of May 1916. For anyone other than Lincoln those would have been dull and depressing months spent locked in a comfortless cell in New York's Raymond Street prison. But although he was theoretically a prisoner, actually he was often seen drinking in saloons, dining with girl friends at expensive restaurants, and giving interviews in newspaper offices.

It was, of course, proper that he should have been treated in America—as in similar circumstances he would have been treated in Britain—with the leniency accorded to a prisoner not yet proved guilty of any crime. But it is a measure of his undoubted personal charm that he managed to secure for himself privileges that went beyond the limits of ordinary prudence—almost beyond the limits of sanity—on the part of the officials whom he bedazzled with his brilliance.

Firstly he demanded that he be allowed to finish writing his book, which was agreed. Then—since the story of his adventures as a spy was the product not of his memory or even of his imagination but of researches at the public library—he demanded access for research purposes to records in the Federal Building, and accommodation in a United States marshal's office where he could write in peace and quietness. This also was agreed.

Then, when his book was completed, his offer to assist the United States Government in decoding German secret messages was accepted; some intercepted documents were given to him, and he played for time until the inevitable day should come when he would have to admit that his knowledge of Intelligence codes would have disgraced the youngest member of a schoolboy secret society.

This farcical situation is comparable with an alien prisoner

on remand in London's Brixton Prison being escorted
daily to the British Museum and afterwards to a quiet office
in Scotland Yard, so that he could earn himself some money
by writing sensational nonsense for sale to Fleet Street; and
afterwards being given similar privileges while he grappled
hopelessly with secret enemy documents handed to him by
friendly and unsuspicious officers of MI5. Senior CID
officers would no doubt agree that it could not happen here!

Most men would have been satisfied with such privileges,
but not Lincoln. He wanted more. As technically a prisoner,
he was escorted on his expeditions by a deputy marshal.
And he soon persuaded his escort that it would be quite
pleasant and could not do any harm if, on their way to and
from Raymond Street, they popped into a few saloons for
drinks. Soon he and his escort were not only drinking
together but dining at expensive restaurants. And it was not
long before their dinner-parties became gay and rather noisy
foursomes with a couple of show-girls.

The main drawback to this pleasant round of literary and
social activities was that Lincoln had to suffer the indignity of
being locked up every night. So one evening he left his
escort outside the lavatory of an expensive hotel while he
departed by a back door, and made a leisurely journey to a
New Jersey farm.

His escape, simple as it had been, made headline news.
British authorities were infuriated, and insulted the New
York Police Department by hiring the Pinkerton Detective
Agency to trace the missing man. And the publishers who
planned to issue his book within a few days were delighted
with this free publicity for their new author.

An eventually disastrous result of the newspaper headlines,
however, was that the German farmer with whom he had

taken refuge began to blackmail him. So on several occasions
Lincoln had to take the risk of returning to New York, where
a red-faced Police Department was waiting to pounce,
visiting the office of the *New York World*, and raising funds
by dictating his outspoken comments on the situation. On
his last visit he was recognized and arrested.

On May 1st, 1916, an American court decided in favour of
Britain on the extradition question. And at the end of that
month he sailed for England in the custody of Chief Inspec-
tor Ward of Scotland Yard.

A feature of the British judicial system which amazes
foreigners is its speed. Exactly a month after he had landed at
Liverpool, and after he had made two preliminary appearances
at Bow Street, London, Lincoln's trial opened at the Old
Bailey on July 4th. The basis of his feeble defence was that
he had been "framed up" on the forgery charge in order that
the British Government should be able to bring him back
from America to face the non-extraditable charge of espionage. What the jury thought of him is indicated by the fact
that they found him guilty without troubling to leave the
box. He received concurrent sentences of three years'
imprisonment on each of several charges.

While he was in prison his certificate of naturalization was
cancelled. When his sentence expired he was not immediately
released and deported to Hungary, as that might have amoun-
ted to sending him to his death. Much had happened while
Lincoln had been in Parkhurst Prison. There had been the
Russian Revolution, and efforts to spread Communism to
other countries in the unsettled conditions of post-War
Europe; in Hungary there had been the brief Communist
regime of Béla Kun, followed by the violently reactionary
and anti-Semitic "White Terror" under the Regent, Admiral

Horthy. It was not until mid-August 1919 that it was deemed safe to send Lincoln back to the country of his birth, and he was put on to a boat crowded with released prisoners that sailed from Harwich to Rotterdam.

Practically penniless—and now stateless—Lincoln secured free transport to Berlin by mixing as a German with his fellow-passengers. In the capital he lived meagrely by selling a few newspaper articles and borrowing money from former contacts. Then, while brooding on his hard luck in an Unter den Linden café one night, he met and became friendly with an Army officer named Colonel Bauer—a casual contact that had the fantastic sequel that six months later Lincoln became a high official of the Government of Germany!

It is hardly possible to summarize the political situation in Germany in those days. Within President Ebert's Second Reich were powerful militant parties—many in uniform— which included, among others, the Spartacists (Communists), the Stahlhelm (ex-Service men), the Reichsbanner Black-Red-Gold (Monarchists), the National Union (reactionaries under Field-Marshal Ludendorff, who seemed to favour placing the ex-Crown Prince Wilhelm Hohenzollern on the throne), and an apparently negligible handful of anti-Semitic nuisances in Munich calling themselves the National Socialist German Workers' Party. These last were inspired by the hysterical oratory of a new member, sent into the movement as a police-spy to report on its activities. His name appeared in British newspapers as "Hittler", but the correct spelling became more familiar later.

Lincoln's new friend Bauer was a typical Prussian officer. He was in close touch with Ludendorff, whose war record placed him high in the esteem of post-War Germany, second only to the father-figure of Field-Marshal von Hindenburg.

I think I should here pause to set the record right for future historians of international Secret Service. My old friend Bernard Newman has told us in his books *Spy* and *Secret Servant* of the Intelligence work he did in Germany at about that time under the alias of "Neumann". His perilous missions took him frequently into Berlin's famous Adlon Hotel and out by a back door. During the same period the same back door was frequently used by Trebitsch Lincoln, accompanied by a rather mysterious figure who led the National Union conspiracy and was known as "Newman". This was an alias used by Field-Marshal Erich von Ludendorff, and Bernard assures me that he did *not* in fact act as Chief of Staff to the German Army during the First World War, did *not* organize a German Monarchist conspiracy, and that Erich von Ludendorff was *not* an alias of Bernard Newman (or Neumann)!

Lincoln was in touch with Ludendorff because he had perceived openings in the National Union for an ambitious man. He soon talked his way into the inner circle of the movement, where Wolfgang Kapp—the puppet leader activated by strings secretly pulled by Ludendorff—described Lincoln as the "spiritual leader" of the party.

It requires a very vivid imagination to picture the secret meetings of the leaders of the National Union conspiracy. A small audience of high-ranking Prussian officers was sternly told—and meekly accepted—what they must do by a stateless adventurer of Hungarian origin who, only a few weeks earlier, had been a convicted forger and swindler in an English prison!

In mid-March 1920 the people of Berlin saw a good deal of marching in and out of the city by columns of troops who were ignorant of why or by whom their orders had been given, or that they were being used for political purposes by a small group of solemnly half-crazy officers. Almost before the general public realized what was happening National Union leaders were installed in Government offices in the Wilhelmstrasse, Wolfgang Kapp assumed the office of Chancellor, and his admired and trusted colleague Trebitsch Lincoln called a Press conference. Such was the bloodless and briefly successful "Kapp *Putsch*".

Foreign correspondents who attended the conference were staggered to find that the Minister who addressed them, and who held among other high offices that of Press Censor, was Trebitsch Lincoln. He drastically altered their reports, cutting out all references to himself, but smuggled reports soon reached Britain. And the British High Commissioner for Occupied Germany gave Chancellor Kapp some startling details about his Press Censor's criminal record. But he need not have troubled to do so, as the opposition of other parties and a general strike by workers caused the collapse of the Kapp regime within a few days.

Restored to power, the Ebert Government issued warrants for the arrest of the National Union conspirators, and Lincoln fled to Budapest and thence to Vienna. Hampered as he so often was by shortage of money, he visited several foreign embassies to try to sell the secret plans of the Monarchists. He raised a small sum, but much less than he had hoped, and the main result of his efforts was to add to his growing list of enemies his former Monarchist colleagues, who made plans to murder him. After a brief period in an Austrian prison he realized that he had no future in Europe, and managed to escape to America, entering the country under a false name.

For a time he worked in a small business run by one of his

brothers in New York. But the authorities traced him at last, and served him with a deportation order. In Britain he would at once have been escorted to a ship by detectives—by force if necessary—and seen safely out of the country. But Lincoln seems to have been left to make his own arrangements, and he did not hurry. By August he had travelled no farther from New York than California, after which there were traces of him in Tokyo in September, and in Shanghai and Chungking.

Lincoln's exploits in China are only comprehensible— are, indeed, only credible—when viewed against the background of the state of that unhappy country in those early nineteen-twenties. The only prosperous and politically stable areas were such extra-territorial settlements as Hong Kong and Shanghai. Much of the remainder of what is virtually a subcontinent, with its hundreds of millions of people, was repeatedly ravaged by the numerous, mutually antagonistic so-called 'war-lords'. These led armies which varied greatly in size and quality, recruited from among scores of millions of starving and illiterate peasant youths, who would have fought for any leader who promised them a few daily handfuls of rice. The ambition of most war-lords was to recruit European advisers, as the most successful armies were those which had been organized and disciplined by ex-officers of various nationalities, who in the shambles of Flanders had learned the dreadful trade which was the only one they knew.

There could have been no more hopeful area in all the world at that time for the undoubted talents of Trebitsch Lincoln. He plunged into the miasmic morass of Chinese politics, and chose as the first victim of his line of sales-talk a minor war-lord, General Yang Sen. Without going into disagreeable details of his past he mentioned to the General that the name of Lincoln had been a powerful one in pre-War Britain and post-War Germany, as well as a name which commanded uncountable dollars in American journalism. And he put forward a sensible and practical suggestion. He hinted delicately that, as leader of a small and relatively inglorious army, the General was never likely to be a great figure in Chinese history; that his best course would be to enter into an alliance with the much more powerful Marshal Wu Pei Fu, so that together they could crush all the other war-lords one by one and eventually govern a united and pacified China.

Yang Sen was impressed: Lincoln busily shuttled back and forth across war-torn ricefields; a treaty was signed; and almost within weeks of his deportation from America Lincoln was political adviser to a powerful combination of warring factions. Once again this incredible man had fallen on his feet.

Just one year after Lincoln's deportation from America a delegation from China arrived unobtrusively in Italy with the object of borrowing European money and personnel. It was led by a brisk and businesslike individual who had a generous expense fund, a pocketful of false passports, and who was—can we not see it coming!—Trebitsch Lincoln.

There was a happy reunion with Gretchen and the boys, a hopeful conference with the international financier Hugo Stinnes, and a meeting with Colonel Bauer, who agreed to accept a military post in China. A few months later the reunited Lincoln family were in a luxury liner on their way to their new home in Nanking. It was unfortunate that Hugo Stinnes had withdrawn his offer of a loan, but Lincoln had secured a similar offer from what turned out to be a sort of back-street Austrian bucket-shop: it was unfortunate that Bauer was not with them, but he had promised to visit China as soon as he had completed an assignment as military adviser to the Red Army in Russia. On the strength of these dubious achievements Lincoln hoped to convey the impression to the war-lords that his European negotiations had had a triumphant success.

But months passed without cash or recruits arriving from Europe, and Lincoln was sent back with orders to produce results, or else. This time he went to Switzerland, but again luck was against him, and he was eventually recalled to China in disgrace. Out of favour with the war-lords, he took his family back to Europe, left them in Germany, and went to New York.

And now for once it is possible to feel a little sorry for Lincoln. The over-active, over-worked brain began to slow down; the resilient, optimistic spirit reeled under a series of blows dealt by Fate—blows that had not always been deserved. He lost hope and lost weight. At the early age of forty-five he seemed to be ready to give up the struggle for wealth and fame, and now to seek no more than a little peace. How he scraped a living in America during that period of despair is not clear. But it is known that his thoughts turned towards religion, preferably of some quiet, contemplative Eastern variety.

Somehow he raised enough money to make his way via China to Ceylon, where he arrived towards the end of 1925. He attached himself to a Buddhist monastery and adopted the name of Chao Kung. Photographs which survive show an austere and shaven but still keen-eyed figure in flowing robe and skullcap.

So the restless spirit found peace at last. But only for a week or two. Fate was waiting to deal him yet another cruel and undeserved blow. Glancing idly through a newspaper from London one day, he read that his son Nat—his eldest and best beloved—was to be hanged in less than a month's time.

Nat had been for some years a regular soldier in the British Army. One night he and another soldier, named Stewart, had a few drinks, armed themselves with pistols, and set out to burgle a house whose occupant was out for the evening. They broke in, drank beer and spirits they found, but were interrupted by the return of the householder. In a drunken panic Nat fired several shots, then both soldiers fled, leaving their victim dying in the darkness in his garden. Detectives soon traced and identified them, and less than a month later both were tried for murder.

Under British law, if someone were killed as a result of the committing of an illegal act by two or more persons, all were held equally guilty of murder. An outstanding example is that of the Croydon youths Craig and Bentley, who were burgling a local warehouse when police arrived. Craig shot and killed a police-officer, and although Bentley was some little distance away and already in police custody, he was hanged. Craig was too young to be executed and went to prison.

It is accordingly rather surprising that Stewart was found not guilty of murder, receiving a sentence of fourteen years for burglary. Nat was sentenced to death.

One of the few decent traits in Lincoln's complex character was his love of children, particularly his own children and, of these, particularly his eldest son, Nat. At once the penniless Buddhist borrowed some money and sailed for England to do what little he could for his son. In the meantime Gretchen had already arrived in England on a similar errand. Lincoln sailed from Colombo on February 5th, 1926, planning to disembark at Marseilles, whence he would just have time to take a train across France and reach England before Nat was executed on March 2nd.

But for some unknown reason the ship's itinerary was altered, and it did not call at Marseilles. So at eight o'clock on the morning of March 2nd Lincoln was staring northwards across the grey sea towards the island he had first come to love and then come to hate—the island where at that moment they were killing his son. His emotions must have placed a strain on his newly acquired Buddhist philosophy.

Disembarking in Holland, Lincoln at once asked for permission to visit Nat's grave. But in Britain executed criminals are buried in a prison yard, with only initials to mark the spot. Their graves are understandably not allowed to become places of pilgrimage. So Lincoln was refused entry into England, and later even refused entry into Germany. He cabled for Gretchen, who met him briefly in Amsterdam. There the mother who had just lost a son learned that she must now face losing her husband. The Buddhist Chao Kung told her that he could not possibly live with a wife.

From this point we need feel no further sympathy for Lincoln. For a man without responsibilities to take refuge from an unkind world in the contemplative existence of a Buddhist monk would be harmless, howsoever futile. But Lincoln had a wife and family whom for the past ten years he had never properly supported and seldom even seen. If he had now determined to go straight it would have been more to his credit if he had stayed with his wife and found some sort of honest work to support her. By taking cowardly shelter under the Buddhist robe he now forced her to start earning her own living again in poorly paid work as a domestic servant.

But, having got rid of Gretchen, he did not immediately

E

return to the monastery, as he had told her he must do. He sold a series of articles about himself to a newspaper, pottered about in Amsterdam and Hamburg for nearly six months, then sailed not for the quiet Colombo countryside, but for the roaring city of New York—an unlikely place, it might seem, in which to try to spread the gentle doctrine of Gautama Buddha. A month or two later he turned up in San Francisco and, in defiance of a promise he had given to the State Department, gave a series of public lectures on Buddhism.

This time he remained in America for over a year, but the authorities forced him to leave at last. Thereafter for years he lived what must have been an impecunious and miserable existence. He was hounded out of every country in which he attempted to take refuge, including successively China, Manchuria, Holland, and France.

An ironical episode occurred when during his enforced travels he met his old friend Bauer, who suggested that Lincoln should work for his own employer, the now powerful war-lord Chiang Kai-Shek—a complete reversal of the situation at their previous meeting. Lincoln declined, and it is a measure of his political acumen that he prophesied that China would eventually become united, but under a Communist Government, and that Chiang Kai-Shek would become no more than an exiled reactionary. Few of even the shrewdest statesmen of those days were capable of seeing so far and so accurately twenty years ahead.

It would become monotonous to follow all the movements of this Hungarian adventurer. Eventually he slipped back into China, and in May 1931 was formally ordained as the Venerable Abbot Chao Kung. He never returned to Ceylon, but it seemed that he could never keep away from Europe for long. Optimistically assuming, perhaps, that his new dignity would secure him greater consideration, he made his way to France, and we next hear of him being pushed out of that country in the autumn of 1932, being refused a visa for Britain, being deported from Belgium, and, on reaching Germany, being thrown into prison for a ten-year-old debt.

He returned to Shanghai, enrolled about a dozen European Buddhist dupes in something he called the "League of Truth", and in the spring of 1934 the venerable and indomitable abbot made one final, futile effort to reach Europe and end his days in that ungrateful continent. He led his League across the Pacific to Canada and thence to England, sending a friendly and forgiving cablegram to the British Prime Minister *en route*. But the forgiveness was not mutual, and on arrival at Liverpool Lincoln was kept in prison until the ship sailed back to Canada. His last few steps on European soil were across the Liverpool landing-stage between two detectives.

Back in Shanghai at last, the membership of the League seems to have dwindled through desertion, disillusionment, and suicide. But the Abbot Chao Kung survived, and somehow paid his way with funds from some untraceable source, believed locally to be the Japanese Secret Service.

During those late nineteen-thirties Imperialist Japan had embarked on vast plans for dominating Asia. Undefended Chinese cites were being bombed and looted, Europeans in the international settlements were being 'debagged' and made to 'lose face' by being paraded through the streets without their trousers. But the arrogant Japs were greatly hampered by an Intelligence service which was effective in China, where any coolie or rickshaw boy might be a Japanese agent, but which could only be effective among

Europeans with the help of hired traitors. In the Western world a Briton like Sidney Reilly could for years pass successfully as a Russian commissar; a Russian like the officer known as "Gordon Lonsdale" could for years pass successfully as a Canadian businessman; but for obvious physical reasons a Japanese Intelligence officer could not possibly pass as a European, and had to try to collect information of use to Tokyo by hiring the scrapings of the Western underworld. So it is not only likely that Japanese agents would have approached a man with Lincoln's talents and experience, but it is likely that—knowing him as we now do—he would have eagerly accepted.

There is no doubt that Lincoln began to comment enthusiastically on the 'pacifying' mission of the brutal Japanese soldiery who were massacring inoffensive Chinese peasants, and it was this that gave support to the widely held belief that the man who had never been a spy for the Germans had become at last a spy for the Japanese. And a few years later, early in the Second World War, he was believed to be one of the group of Western traitors who broadcast Japanese propaganda.

So it seems possible that, had he survived the War, Lincoln might have been brought to trial as a war criminal with "Tokyo Rose" and others. But during the night of October 9th, 1942, Ignatius Timothy Trebitsch Lincoln, *alias* the Venerable Abbot Chao Kung, *alias* scores of other names, died in a Shanghai hospital.

VI

I revert finally to the Kapp *Putsch* in Germany in 1920. An insignificant new party in Bavaria had promised its support, and its leaders were expected in Berlin. When the *Putsch* failed Lincoln rushed to the airfield to warn the conspirators and to save them from arrest.

An aircraft arrived, and a man got out. Lincoln promptly bundled him back into the cabin and told him to return to Bavaria or he would be summarily arrested and face a serious sentence. Thus the man had another thirteen years to prepare his own *Putsch*, for his name was Adolf Hitler.

FOUR

The Trial of Mrs O'Grady

I

THE 'SCISSORS-AND-PASTE' BOOK is well known in publishing. Competently done, it can be very interesting—and successful. The author is usually a journalist; he collects Press reports on, say, a series of murders, outlines the stories, emphasizes any outstanding features, maybe adds a few comments—and often quite a lot of imaginative embroidery. Murder is the most popular subject, but espionage follows it closely.

The subject lends itself to this treatment. True, the writer makes much use of the time-honoured clichés. For example, every woman spy is by definition beautiful. She is dangerous—she seduces statesmen and generals into betraying their secrets—not the office, but the bedchamber, is her workroom.

A number of books—almost the whole of those covering cases of women spies—have included chapters on Mrs Dorothy Pamela O'Grady, who was sentenced to death in February 1941. I summarize one of these, with the comment that it is no worse than many of the others.

According to these legends, Mrs O'Grady appeared in the Isle of Wight in the late nineteen-thirties. It was not known whence she came, but she acquired British nationality by marrying an Englishman—a favourite device of German women agents. She had been recruited by Marianne Ennig, the lover of Dr Hermann Goertz, who had been caught and sentenced as a spy in 1936. Despite his failure, Fräulein Ennig taught his methods to Mrs O'Grady.

The latter acquired a boarding-house in Sandown—it was never discovered whence she got the money. Her guests were exclusively Germans!

Mrs O'Grady was a good amateur artist, and liked to tramp the countryside with her sketching equipment. Strangely, the places she favoured were those where new—and then highly secret—radar stations were being erected.

The war began, and the Isle of Wight was important in the defence of Britain. Mrs O'Grady was trailed—not only on her country walks, but on her frequent journeys to London—where she visited an address already under suspicion; she also travelled to Portsmouth and Southampton.

In the files of MI5 she was known as "Sweet Rosie O'Grady". At last the Special Branch moved in. Hidden among the springs of easy-chairs and behind false backs to drawers in her home they found sketches of radar installations, anti-tank fortifications, with maps showing gun sites and plans of naval dockyards. It was proved that she had even cut the cables connecting the Isle of Wight with the mainland—which might have led to disaster in the event of a German invasion.

In the dock she faced her accusers calmly. One writer has written: "I do not think that I was the only man in that courtroom to feel ungrudging admiration for the tall, eloquent woman who conducted herself in court with great skill and courage and who put up such a desperate fight for life."

She was found guilty and condemned to death. On appeal the capital sentence was reduced to one of fourteen years' imprisonment. "However, two years after the War ended she was released, and returned to Germany."

This, I repeat, is a fair specimen of the stories published about Mrs O'Grady—one of them, in a popular weekly magazine, as recently as 1962. But the account from which I have quoted is sadly inaccurate, though correct in its statement that "She was found guilty and condemned to death."

The writer to whom I have referred must have been singularly unobservant. He was present at her trial, and describes her as tall and eloquent: actually she was short, dumpy—and never said a word except "Not guilty".

I can myself counter his last sentence. She was released five years after the War ended, but she did *not* return to Germany. She had never been there in her life—had never been anywhere abroad. After her release she returned to her home in the Isle of Wight—where I spent several hours with her the day before writing this chapter.

II

She was no German, but a Londoner, born near Clapham Common. She married a man of Irish. stock, as his name suggests. He was a fireman; his grandfather had been a 'Peeler' in the days when policemen wore tall hats.

She opened her boarding-house in Sandown in 1932. I

examined her visitors' book—not a German name and address in it; instead, notes from lodgers praising her friendly hospitality. These I could believe, for she is a homely woman, her mass of hair now grey; still short, naturally, and now rather stout: a glint in her eyes suggested a keen sense of humour. They give her trouble, nevertheless, and she needs glasses; she is also afflicted by attacks of arthritis.

Her husband was twenty years older than herself, and when war broke out he had retired. However, he returned to the fire service, and worked gallantly through the London blitz. The couple had no children, and Mrs O'Grady devoted her affection to dogs. It was a black retriever, Rob, who inadvertently led her into trouble.

I made full notes of our conversation, and think it best to tell her story in her own words—adding my own comments in brackets. I found her account quite fascinating—not as a spy story, but as a study which a psychologist would value.

"All my life, since I was a child, I have loved to make up stories and pretend I have been or done all sorts of things that I had not done, out of a love of shocking people," she began. "I used to love to shock people and pretend I was ever so bad. As a child at school I remember writing on bits of paper and signing them with my name, saying that I had killed my mother. I hid the notes all about the place hoping they would be found and that I would be hanged. I was then about twelve years old. My mother had died a year earlier—and actually I was very fond of her.

"When the War began my husband was posted to London. Rob was my only companion. He loved to swim in the sea, but the beach at Sandown was closed. So I used to take Rob further along the cliffs, where we could get down to the sea.

I walked miles to get the better of the soldiers in order to reach the beach.

"One day I was near Whitecliff Bay. There was a public path going down the slope—no barbed wire across it, and no notice forbidding entry. So I followed the path. Rob had his swim, and I paddled. Then I sat down, reading a book and eating an apple. A sergeant and a soldier came along, and said that I was in a prohibited place, right under their secret guns. I was scared—I don't like bangs.

"Then the soldier noticed a little swastika flag under my lapel. I had a large map of Europe at home, and used to stick in flags to show the battle line. Evidently one of the German flags had got caught in my hair. I had found it there as I walked, so I pinned it under my lapel. Then the soldiers saw it, and they told me that I must go with them to their headquarters. They must have thought I was a spy."

(Presumably a soldier would know that a German spy does *not* go about wearing a swastika flag! But these were nervous days: August 1940. A German invasion was expected day by day, and the Isle of Wight was a pivot of British defensive schemes. Everybody was on the alert, and the imagination was stirred by the peril of the moment. The atmosphere led to fantasies—as when the Home Guard rang church bells, believing that the invasion had begun.)

"It was a very hot day, and I did not want to walk all that way. So I made to move off. The sergeant shouted, 'Halt, or I fire!' I was thrilled—this was real excitement.

"Then I did a silly thing, I admit. I felt sorry for the soldiers—I had often taken out a cup of tea or a cigarette to sentries near my house. So now I took a ten-shilling note from my purse and said, 'I'm sorry to have bothered you. Buy some cigarettes with this.'

"Instead they marched me off to their officer. He was very nice, and gave me chocolates. But the sergeant told him that he had found me in a secret place, and that I had tried to bribe him to let me go.

"The officer did let me go, but evidently he reported the incident to the police. A very young constable came round to see me, and asked for my views on Hitler. I was flattered, and told him a lot of nonsense. I said that Hitler was a great man. Why shouldn't he take Poland, I asked. Hadn't we taken other countries in our time? I said that the war was a lot of nonsense—men playing at being soldiers.

"The policeman was very serious, and took it all down."

(He must have been *very* young. The spy often uses patriotism as a disguise—he would never reveal himself so blatantly.)

"I was quite excited. They seemed to think that I was a spy! I thought what fun it would be to *pretend* to be a spy. I thought out all the things that a spy would do, and tried to do them. I drew little sketch-maps, and dropped them where I thought soldiers would find them."

(Mrs O'Grady was *not* an artist. Her sketches were crude— she used the maps from the guide-book or a bus timetable, marking in real or imaginary defence posts. Her ideas as to what a spy would do were derived exclusively from popular thrillers—*not* a very accurate source.)

"But nothing happened for weeks. I had almost forgotten the incident with Rob on the beach, when all of a sudden I got a summons, ordering me to appear on a charge of being in a prohibited place and attempting to bribe the guards.

"I thought, 'Why should I go to court? I've done nothing wrong. To hell with them.' So I decided to take a holiday: I packed a bag and went to Totland Bay. There by accident

I met a woman who lived alone: she was so deaf that she couldn't hear the siren or the all-clear, so she was glad to have me live with her, so that I could tell her."

(But, of course, the police had interpreted her flight as a proof of guilt—as, indeed, she probably intended.)

"It was all very thrilling—I guessed that there would be a warrant out for my arrest, and that the police would be searching for me because I had not gone to the court.

"But I was getting bored at not being able to play at spying. I left some swastikas in my bedroom. There the deaf woman found them, and she told the police. So I was taken off. In my handbag they found a plan, which I kept there to prove that I was a spy.

"The police said I had better have a solicitor, so my husband engaged Mr Palmer. He was a nice old silly. He said, 'Oh, we'll soon have you out of this.' I thought, 'Oh, will you!' So I tried to make him believe that I really was a spy.

"The police questioned me for hours, and took down everything I said. I admitted everything, and added more. They were so serious, but I was laughing inside. They wanted to know how I got my information to Germany, and I told them that a man landed in a rubber dinghy from a submarine. I had read that in a book.

"You do understand what I was doing? It had all become a huge joke. You write stories—I was *living* one. In my imagination I *was* a spy. I had always been a nobody; now I was somebody, with people taking notice of me. I had loved creating a mystery. It was like living in a novel in real life."

(I might not understand fully, but I knew that her near-hallucination was not uncommon. In fiction, I thought of the stories of Walter Mitty and Billy Liar. In fact, there was the recent case of Bryan Scott. He had been released from the

Royal Navy on medical grounds; in a coffee bar in Chelsea
he met Stewart Gunther-Rains. To him he pretended to be a
Russian—Nikolai Bryanovitch Petrov. He produced a revolver; he said that he had made a secret journey from Holland,
and claimed to be an "international agent", ready for anything from spying to killing. He displayed pages of complicated electronic information marked "Secret".

Gunther-Rains naturally went to the police, and Scott
was arrested. But he was no spy. "A bad detective story",
"A comic opera performance"—these were phrases used at
his trial. It was a case of overdrawn imagination. Scott had
apparently taken the idea from a book by an old friend of
mine, the Russian Colonel Victor Kaledin: *K14—OM66—
Adventures of a Double Spy*.

But the electronic documents were genuine. Scott had
wrongfully retained them when he left his post as a Naval
radio operator. For this he was fined £40 and costs at Marl-
borough Street Police Court, London.

The records of MI5 and the Special Branch contain
details of hundreds of similar cases. And how often have the
police been bothered by men who confess falsely—to
murder?

But we must return to Mrs O'Grady, now committed for
trial.)

"The police had made a fuss about my identity card. I
really did lose this, and had to get another one from the
town hall. Then my first card turned up in an old coat. So I
rubbed out the name and address on one of the cards, put in
ones I had made up, and altered the identity letters and
numbers. A spy must have a false identity card!

"It was very useful to show to the soldiers whenever I took
Rob to the beach for his swim. I used to say that I was a

visitor from London—and show my forged card—and did not know that I must not go down on the beach. Then they used to be nice to me. They would have been cross with me if they had known that I lived on the island.

"I had told my solicitor that I had been a spy, as the police said, and I was thrilled and delighted when he said that I might be condemned to death. But I intended to tell my counsel. My idea was that I would tell the whole truth when I got into the witness-box.

"But when I told this to my solicitor I don't think he really believed me. He believed that I had already told the truth, and that when I went into the witness-box I was going to tell a pack of lies.

"I think that perhaps he must have told this to my counsel, Mr Scott Henderson. I only saw him for a couple of minutes. He came rushing in and said, 'I am in a great hurry. I am due in another case. But you must understand, Mrs O'Grady, that I will not be a party to perjury—I will not act on your behalf unless you agree *not* to go into the witness-box.' Well, what could I do? He produced a paper, and I signed it. But I still believed that I had a *right* to give evidence on my own behalf.

"Before the trial, while I was in Holloway, the Head of MI5 came to see me. He wanted to know who my contact was, and how I met him. He did not seem to believe my story about the man from the submarine."

(Of course he didn't. No sensible man would. It was sheer cloak-and-dagger melodrama, a feature of long outdated spy fiction. I know on the best of evidence that he was uneasy about the whole case, but he had to pursue it. Unlikely though it seemed, he *had* known more fantastic stories with some basis of truth.)

"Then came my trial, at Winchester. It was secret [i.e., *in camera*]. I had looked forward to it as a tremendous thrill. It lasted two days.

"But I don't remember very much about it. The two women officers from Aylesbury who sat with me in the dock were very nice, and kept whispering to me to keep my spirits up. So I didn't hear very much of what was being said in court. In fact, I was very surprised when I learned later that I had been charged with cutting telephone wires, and had confessed to it. An Army officer described what had been done, but he didn't say that *I* had done it. I would not have cut any wires, of course. I would never have done anything which I thought would do harm to my country."

(*Not* cables to the mainland. The charge specifically stated: "That with intent to help the enemy she committed an act designed to impede the military operations of H.M. Forces by cutting a military telephone."

Other charges referred to plans she had made "likely to give assistance to the military operations of the enemy", and of conspiring with persons unknown to convey information to the enemy.)

"I can make a good guess who did cut the wire. One day, when I was out with Rob, I saw an errand boy behaving very suspiciously. There were telephone lines all over the place. The soldiers didn't put them on poles, but hung them on hedges, and so on.

"They called soldiers to prove that I had been on the beach, and police to say that I had confessed to all sorts of things. But some of the evidence bewildered me. Rob was a big dog, young and headstrong. He used to chase seagulls— he often frightened me by stopping dead on the very edge of the cliff. And now a woman gave evidence that she had seen me walking along the cliffs, and that I kept looking around and behind me. Of course I was. I was keeping an eye on Rob.

"Well, my counsel wouldn't let me go into the witness-box, so I had no chance to tell the truth. I have forgotten what he talked about in his speech. The other counsel said that because of my maps the defence plans for the island had had to be changed.

"The excitement of being tried for my life was intense. The supreme moment came when an official stood behind the judge and put on his black cap for him before pronouncing the death sentence.

"The man didn't put it on straight. It went over one of the judge's eyes and looked so funny that I was giggling inside and had a job not to laugh. It was hard to keep a straight face and look serious and solemn, as I knew a spy should. I was shaking with laughter inside me, although I cried a lot when I got downstairs.

"But it had been so thrilling. The judge gave the whole of the death sentence. I thought that nowadays they only read a bit of it, but he did the lot—what was to happen to my body, and so on. It was very exciting. I was now living in a real-life drama, and no mistake about it.

"I found it disappointing that I was going to be hanged instead of shot. I thought spies were always shot. But I had always wanted to see what happened when they hanged somebody.

"My next disappointment was to learn that they would put a hood over my head and tie my hands behind my back before they took me to the scaffold. I said, 'What is the good of being hanged if I can't see what's happening?'

"I spent Christmas in the death cell. They gave me a little piece of Christmas cake and a few sweets.

"And sometimes I said, 'They won't hang a woman in England.' "

When her husband visited her—for all she knew, for the last time—one of the thoughts uppermost in her mind was for her dog. She had left money and her own meat coupons with a butcher to feed him. "Don't let anybody else have him. If you can't keep him, have him put to sleep. He can't live alone—there would be nobody to save him if the house was bombed!"

III

But not even the morbid experience of a death sentence had cured Mrs O'Grady's over-vivid imagination. Women officers sat in the cell with her, and she still continued to spin her yarns about her spying activities. These were duly written down.

"My only fear was that I would be taken away one morning to be hanged without having been told the night before. Sometimes I dreaded going to sleep in case this happened. I was terrified—yet I enjoyed being terrified."

The Court of Criminal Appeal quashed the sentence on the grounds of the learned judge's misdirection to the jury. He had laid undue stress on "communicating information to the enemy", and there was not a scrap of evidence that she had done anything of the kind—for, of course, the man from a submarine could not be produced as a witness, as he did not even exist. But Mrs O'Grady was sentenced to fourteen years' imprisonment on the other charges—penetrating into prohibited places, making maps which could be useful to the enemy, and cutting a military telephone wire. So she went to Aylesbury prison.

F

She spoke very highly of the officials there, and especially of Dame Lilian Barker, of the Prison Commission, who often visited her. But she had soon tired of prison life—naturally, for she was a respectable woman who had lived in reasonable comfort.

The time came when she decided to tell the whole story to her long-suffering husband. She wrote down what was in effect a synopsis of what I have recorded here: it is on my desk as I write.

A woman prisoner was due for release. She volunteered to smuggle out the story—it covered ten pages of an exercise book—hidden under her breasts. But a prison officer discovered it.

Now the secret was out. The whole episode was revealed as a 'joke'. I know that many of the Security staff were relieved that Mrs O'Grady had not been hanged. They had always been uneasy, for the evidence was too flimsy. Had it not been for Mrs O'Grady's confessions the charges could never have stood up.

Later Mrs O'Grady was persuaded to petition for a pardon. It was refused. Her story might be true—indeed, it was proved to be true—but by her folly she had undoubtedly forced an expensive realignment of the Isle of Wight's defences. (Surely, too, her case had taught some elementary lessons to the local Security officers!)

Her husband had stood by her loyally: he was getting old, and she wanted to look after him. So, in November 1949, she made a desperate appeal to the Home Secretary. This time he decided that she had been adequately punished for her folly. So early in 1950 she was released. She returned home, and reopened her boarding-house.

She sold her story to the *Sunday Express* for £75. ("I am

no Christine Keeler," she said, laughing). We can reasonably reprimand the scissors-and-paste authors who still tell her story up to the point of her trial, but not beyond. Anyone who knew the least thing about Intelligence should have noticed the flimsy character of the evidence against her. And her release was not kept secret. Early in 1950 I published a book which was serialized in a very popular weekly. It contained an adequate account of the O'Grady case. And the *Sunday Express* has a wide circulation!

"Did you just tell your story to a journalist?" I asked.

"No. I gave him a copy of the account I wrote to my husband while I was in Aylesbury Gaol."

"Was it embellished?"

"No. He embroidered it with one or two phrases, but in effect it is accurate. It is the same story that I have told to you this afternoon in greater detail. It is the true story."

"Why did you do this foolish thing? Why did you begin the fake?"

"Well, I had never been anything in all my life. I have always been insignificant. I never had a close friend, even at school.

"I felt tremendously bucked when I saw that they thought I was clever enough to be a spy. I had been so long an ordinary seaside landlady—now I was someone in the public eye. It made me feel important."

There it is, that mental kink which protrudes through every incident of the record. No dangerous German spy, but "an ordinary seaside landlady", longing to be "someone", and in her imagination fulfilling her ambitious impulses.

Mrs O'Grady was foolish. She asked for trouble, and got it. But she has paid for her folly, and surely now she deserves freedom from libel.

Her story is far removed from an epic of espionage. When I first wrote about Mrs O'Grady I said that hers was obviously a case of great interest to a psychiatrist. My typist slipped over the last word, and made it spychiatrist.

FIVE

Burgess minus Maclean

I

IN APRIL 1962 I was lecturing in Lancashire. As I walked from the platform a man from BBC Television awaited me.

"I have a car outside," he said. "Can I take you to our studio in Manchester?"

"Yes. Why?"

"Our people want you to do a commentary during the News."

"On what?"

"I believe that Burgess and Maclean are on their way to England."

"Right. Let's go."

To me the news seemed incredible. The return of Burgess was comprehensible. There was no direct evidence of espionage against him; he was very fond of his mother, who was ill; and during Mr Macmillan's visit to Moscow he had attempted to find out if he might return to England.

Maclean was a very different case. I was quite certain that he would never venture to return.

Yet the information which awaited me in Manchester seemed definite enough. That morning Detective-Superintendent G. G. Smith of the Special Branch, with a representative of the Director of Public Prosecutions, had waited on the Chief Metropolitan magistrate, and had been given a warrant for the arrest of Burgess and Maclean! This was quite different from the popular type of rumour which had for so long bedevilled the case.

News was streaming in. BEA reported that the two men would arrive in Amsterdam by KLM, change planes, and arrive at London Airport by BEA at 10.10 P.M.

Fleet Street prepared for the occasion. Journalists and cameramen were flown to Amsterdam. Hundreds gathered at London Airport, with fast cars to carry pictures to newspaper offices. My doubts began to appear unjustified. Yet I still could not believe the story, and I took a very cautious line in my commentary. Its theme was "What will be the charge against Burgess?"

The warrant for the arrest was issued under Section One of the Official Secrets Act. This covers the gathering of information in prohibited places, the making of plans, sketches, or models, the communication of official codes, ciphers, or passwords, calculated to be, directly or indirectly, useful to an enemy. The charge carries a maximum penalty of fourteen years' imprisonment.

Did Burgess's activities fall under this heading? I did not believe it. Nor did I believe that he—or especially Maclean—would risk a return home.

While the Pressmen were surging around London Airport, Moscow correspondents were also busy. One drove to Maclean's flat. The door was slammed in his face—by Maclean!

Others went to Burgess's apartment. He too was at home. As usual, he was drinking whisky; and, also as usual, he had a 'boy' in attendance.

II

Guy Frances de Moncy Burgess came of a good family: his father was a distinguished naval officer. Guy went to Eton; then, anxious to follow his father, to the Naval College at Dartmouth. There, however, his eyesight was found to be below the high standard required for a naval officer; he was allowed to return to Eton—an unusual privilege, granted because of his exceptional ability.

He moved on to Cambridge, where again he attracted attention. He had a first-class mind, and was a brilliant conversationalist. His tutors forecast a bright future for him, and one of his professors even wished him to become a Fellow of his college. "The most brilliant undergraduate of his time," was the verdict of another.

Years later it was alleged that he had admitted that he had been a Communist while still at Cambridge, but there was no supporting evidence. Certainly he held what would then be classed as Left-wing views. He booed Mr Neville Chamberlain—not without reason, for the Chancellor of the Exchequer, as he then was, claimed that the unemployed suffered no real hardship. He joined the 1934 'hunger march' for one stage: but there were millions of people, non-Communists, whose sympathies lay with the tragic marchers. He expressed anti-Government opinions, but so did plenty of others. He made a holiday visit to Russia, and returned depressed: he had decided that "Communism was in fact a reactionary movement", not the first whose

ideological illusions were shattered by Communist practice.
If he had been a member of the Communist Party he certainly
left it after visiting Moscow.

Indeed, his career had parallels in those of hundreds of
other bright young men of his day. He drank far more than
was good for him, but so did others. He had, however, one
outstanding weakness: he was a homosexual. He never
attempted to disguise it: on occasion he even flaunted his
'lovers' before his friends. This point is of some importance.
Today there is a popular supposition that a homosexual is
likely to be a spy. There is no substance at all in this suggestion. But a homosexual usually hides his failing, lest he should
fall foul of the law, and so a foreign agent who had pene-
trated his secret might blackmail him into service. But
Burgess had no secret, and would have been joyously
delighted at the idea of being blackmailed.

When he left Cambridge he took a job as secretary to a
Conservative Member of Parliament. From this he moved on
to the BBC, where he supervised a well-known programme,
"The Week in Westminster". He was very successful with
this: so many M.P.s are dull and prosy, but Burgess livened
up their talks considerably.

In the course of this work he met many leading politicians
—including Winston Churchill. The great man realized
Burgess's ability, and in a book he presented to him referred
to his "admirable sentiments".

He had other and less reputable acquaintances—apart
from his fellow-homosexuals. He denounced at least one of
them to MI5 as a possible suspect; thereafter he did other odd
jobs for British Security organizations, on a 'payment-by-
results' basis.

In 1938 he left the BBC. A friend had been appointed

head of a new Intelligence section, which was to direct sabotage and propaganda if war began. This sounded exciting, and Burgess was glad to join it. But the section lasted only a few months, and Burgess returned to the BBC.

Now he was put in charge of another popular programme, "Can I help you?" When the War began he arranged a transfer—with the aid of political friends—to the Foreign Office. He held only a junior post—until, after the War, Mr Hector McNeil became Minister of State at the Foreign Office. He had met Burgess in his "Week in Westminster" days; like many others, he was impressed by the man's ability, and appointed him his Personal Assistant.

In 1950 Burgess was posted to the British Embassy in Washington. Although he was in only a low grade, it was an extraordinary appointment. There was never any question about his ability, but a blatant homosexual who was frequently drunk could scarcely be considered suitable for any diplomatic post.

He was soon in trouble. He was careless with confidential papers; he was completely unstable; at the cocktail parties which are a feature of diplomatic life in Washington he talked loudly—and criticized his own Government and that of his hosts. Everybody, it seemed, was wrong but Guy Burgess. He had become involved with a notorious American homosexual—a man with a police record; and he was stopped for dangerous driving, or for driving while under the influence of alcohol. Clearly he was a liability in an embassy, and the Ambassador told him that he was a disgrace to the diplomatic service, and would have to go. So Burgess returned to London in ignominy.

His conduct in America had been quite inexcusable—a flamboyant defiance of all the rules as well as all accepted conventions. He continually attracted attention to himself by his behaviour. Diplomatically this was deplorable—but it was *not* the conduct of a spy. A secret agent is by definition secret—and Burgess was emphatically the reverse.

III

Here it is necessary to insert a brief note on Donald Duart Maclean. He was the son of a highly respected Liberal leader, and had entered the Foreign Service by competitive examination. At Cambridge he had known Burgess, but was never one of his particular friends. He may have been a member of the Communist Party, but only for a short time.

He was highly esteemed at the Foreign Office. He worked hard, and won regular promotions. But he was a psychopath, a 'split personality'. After spells of hard and excellent work he would indulge in a period of drunken violence. His sexual life was peculiar. He had married a charming and intelligent American girl—but when he was drunk he became a homosexual.

After one vicious and violent spell in Cairo he was returned to London. There the Foreign Office had him treated by a psychiatrist for a 'nervous breakdown'.

He had already served in the U.S.A., and was now made head of the American Department of the Foreign Office. Again, this was a peculiar appointment, for Maclean had made no secret of his anti-American views. They were apparently based on the American suspicions of Russia and hatred of Communism.

Now two years earlier, in 1949, the Foreign Office had picked up a hint that a secret document had been handed over to the Russians, and the Security staff instituted an investigation. There were more than 6000 possible culprits, and the check took two years. But by May 1951 the list of suspects had been narrowed to three—one of whom was Maclean.

By this time Burgess was back in London, suspended from duty, and with dismissal imminent. He sought out his former Cambridge contact, and asked Maclean if he were under suspicion of anything: a Security officer in Washington, knowing of their acquaintance, had asked Burgess questions about Maclean. The latter denied that he had done anything which could have prompted suspicion.

But a few days later Burgess returned with some definite information. He had received it through the 'Third Man' in the case.

H. A. R. Philby—known as "Kim"—was the son of a famous expert on Arab affairs. He himself knew the Middle East well. During the War he had given valuable service to Britain's Intelligence organizations. Probably it was not known at that time that he had been an ardent Communist—and, for that matter, still was.

He told Burgess that Maclean was strongly suspected of espionage on behalf of Russia, and would shortly be arrested. Aroused by this information, Maclean made some elementary tests, and discovered that he was indeed being trailed by detectives. He decided to flee the country—and Russia was his obvious choice.

Burgess was about to lose his job—and his dismissal would scarcely help him to find another. He was grossly dissatisfied with his career: he looked upon himself as a man of superior ability who had been forced to work— unhappily—under commonplace chiefs. At the last minute he decided to accompany Maclean; in Russia he would start again. It was as simple as that.

IV

The details of their journey are unimportant—and most of those published were inaccurate. Their flight was *not* organized by the Russians, who were surprised by their arrival in Moscow.

But, once the Russians had accepted the two refugees, the inevitable cloak-and-dagger proceedings were applied. Burgess and Maclean simply disappeared. It was guessed where they had gone, but there was no proof of this. Their families received very occasional letters, posted in different countries—some of them in London. Then in 1953 followed another cloak-and-dagger episode. Mrs Maclean and her children disappeared from Switzerland. It was, of course, assumed that she had gone to join her husband. But where?

The search for Burgess and Maclean had been transferred from the Foreign Office and MI5 to the Press. One enterprising newspaper engaged Lieutenant-Colonel Oreste Pinto, the BBC "Spycatcher", to trace them. His failure was complete. True, he was not really a 'spycatcher', but an admirable interrogator of suspects—a qualification of little value in this case, where the suspects were not available.

The Russians would not admit their arrival; Mr Khrushchev declared that he had never heard of Burgess and Maclean, and later denied outright that they were in the Soviet Union. But in 1956 he was to make a visit to Britain—and was advised that he would be asked endless questions on Burgess and Maclean. So there was arranged what was described as a 'Press conference' at the National Hotel in

Moscow. Four journalists were invited to a certain room—and there Burgess and Maclean awaited them.

The 'conference' was brief. The two men handed out prepared statements, stated that they were well and happy, and promptly disappeared.

After that Burgess was frequently seen by Moscow correspondents. I myself saw him once when on a casual visit to Russia, but unfortunately he was too drunk to be intelligible. Maclean was always less accessible.

The Russians had allocated to the two defectors tasks bearing no relation to espionage: Burgess worked for the Foreign Literature Publishing House, recommending English books for translation into Russian. Maclean had a similar job with another organization which published Russian books in English and other foreign languages.

Visitors, including their own friends, reported that they were not very happy. Considering his unhealthy life, the death of Burgess in 1963, at the age of fifty-two, was not remarkable.

I have always held that the importance of the Burgess-Maclean affair was grossly exaggerated; though an official American publication classes them among the nuclear spies, this is absurd. Yet the episode had important effects on Anglo-American relations. The Americans declared that they had no confidence in British Security measures—though their own were equally suspect. The fact is that no 'loyalty tests' are ever worth very much. Burgess and Maclean had been 'screened' more than once, and had passed without suspicion.

In this book I am concerned primarily with Burgess. Though, as I have said, the Special Branch had reason to believe that Maclean might have been concerned in the earlier leak, there was no such suspicion of his associate. The whole 'case' against him, in fact, depends upon hearsay.

But the Americans denied Britain the use of their Pacific nuclear testing-ground because their Security staff believed that successors to Burgess and Maclean might reveal its secrets to the Russians.

V

Vladimir Petrov was a Soviet official. In 1951 he was ordered to Australia, where his post at the Canberra Embassy was that of Consul and Cultural Attaché. He was then a member of the Russian spy service, but in 1954 he and his wife defected. Their revelations were as important as those of Igor Gouzenko in Canada in 1945, and made the Burgess and Maclean affair appear puny in comparison.[1] He is now quoted as the principal witness against the two British renegades.

One of his subordinates in the Australian branch of the Russian Secret Service was a man named Kislytsin, who had previously worked in the London Embassy. Petrov admits that he himself knew nothing of Burgess and Maclean beyond the newspaper reports of their disappearance, and that all his subsequent information was gained in conversation with Kislytsin.

The latter declared that after the end of the War, when Burgess was Personal Assistant to Mr McNeil at the Foreign Office, he handed over brief-cases of information to the MVD in the Russian Embassy in London, and left official documents there to be photographed. Burgess, he claimed, had been a Russian agent since his Cambridge days.

[1] See *Empire of Fear*, by V. and E. Petrov.

Kislytsin's account contains many obvious inaccuracies, as well as glaring contradictions to Burgess's own statements to visitors in Moscow. But it has been generally accepted as factual.

I must return to the point which opens my chapter. If Burgess were indeed on his way to London he would be arrested on his arrival. On what charge? And confronted with what evidence?

Without doubt he was keenly interrogated by the Russians when he turned up in Moscow. He could have given only a modest amount of information: he had been no more than a junior officer, and such news as he could pick up while assistant to a Minister in the Foreign Office was now seriously out of date. In any event, how could it be *proved* in a court of law that Burgess had passed on any information at all? It was a reasonable assumption that he had, but a trial requires proof. The only people who could supply the necessary evidence were the Russians—who were hardly likely to do so!

Kislytsin's story to Petrov? This could never be admitted as evidence: English law takes no account of hearsay. As the Pickwickian judge said to Sam Weller, "What the soldier said is not evidence." The Kislytsin yarn might arouse suspicion among American Security officers, but it could have no place in a British court of law.

There is no direct evidence whatever against Burgess—indeed, there are many suggestions that he never was a spy. Would the Russians—no amateurs in espionage!—engage a drunken homosexual as an agent? Or, if Burgess were a spy, would he have blatantly called attention to himself by his excesses?

He sneered at the fantastic yarns about his allegedly

imminent return to England. (They appear to have been started off by a remark by Burgess that he would like to take his annual holiday in Cuba.) He blamed the Dutch for the rumours: they needed a fantasy to cover up the case of Alexei Golub—who had defected to Holland but had now decided to retur⟨⟩to Russia. And he claimed that the British Government dared not arrest and try him, for in his defence he would denounce other homosexuals in the Foreign Office!

He died in the country he had chosen, where he had been supplied with or had otherwise acquired a youth as his companion. His drunken conduct was severely criticized in Victorian Russia, and his invitations to parties dwindled to nothing. He was left with his boy-friend, an ample supply of vodka, and a myriad of unhappy memories.

SIX

The Flight of Doctor Pontecorvo

I

THERE IS A POPULAR but absurd superstition that all Communists are Russian spies and that all anti-Fascists are Communists.

Certainly Doctor Bruno Pontecorvo had no reason to love the Fascists. Born in Pisa, Italy, of a respected Jewish family, he took his degree at the University of Pisa and went on to Rome for postgraduate research under the famous Professor Enrico Fermi. There he was one of a group of six which published in 1935 an important scientific article, "Artificial Radioactivity produced by Neutron Bombardment". This opened up new fields for experiments, which in turn led to important advances in nuclear research. Indeed, the six scientists filed a claim against the American Government for ten million dollars for use of their materials and patents.

Mussolini's Italy did not realize the importance of the research, however; and Pontecorvo was Jewish. When anti-Semitic persecution began to intensify he fled to Paris, where he worked under Professor Joliot-Curie. He married a

G 97

Swedish girl, and they escaped from France by bicycle during the Nazi invasion in 1940.

He later emigrated to the U.S.A., and at first worked for an oil company. He proved to be an admirable radiographic oil-well logger, and took out a patent for a new process. Then, at the suggestion of Professor Fermi, the Canadian Government offered him a post in the Anglo-Canadian team of nuclear physicists at Chalk River. He worked hard on heavy-water projects—the approach to the atomic bomb—and paid several visits to American nuclear installations. In 1946 he was transferred to the British Ministry of Supply Atomic Energy Organization, and two years later he was granted British citizenship.

He was a first-class physicist, an outstanding member of what was then a very limited profession. He had become well known within his specialist field, and had been offered several posts—including one of assistant professor at Cornell University at 7000 dollars a year. He chose instead to move to Harwell—as a senior principal scientific officer at £1300 a year—little more than half the American offer. At Harwell he worked on projects concerned with nuclear energy, not with bombs. His work was excellent but *not* secret.

In February 1950 the Fuchs case was pending, and Ponte-corvo went to Wing Commander Henry Arnold, the Security Officer at Harwell. He thought he ought to mention that his younger brother Gilberto was a Communist.

He should have mentioned this earlier—or one of the Security organizations should have found it out. But Ponte-corvo and his brother were not apparently on especially friendly terms, and they had not even met for some time.

True, further inquiry would have revealed that his sister Giuliana was married to a well-known Italian Communist.

However, the rest of his family was beyond reproach. It had split up when Mussolini's heavy hand was displayed in 1938. One brother became a respected professor of biology at Glasgow University, another an agricultural expert in England. One sister became a teacher, another a nurse. At the same time another brother had become a radio specialist in the U.S.A. All had rendered excellent service to their adopted countries, especially during the War.

Bruno worked hard at Harwell, and was popular there. He was dark, good-looking, charming, a good tennis player, carefree, with a keen sense of humour. True, he was casual. He would often turn up late for appointments; and he used to say that he never counted the notes in his wallet so that he would not know if he had lost any—thus he would escape worry!

Doctor Fuchs was also employed at Harwell. The two men met very occasionally, but were not friends—the shy Fuchs had little in common with the lively Pontecorvo.

The latter had three children. The family were never known to talk politics. (Later, Fuchs expressed his surprise that Pontecorvo could have had any connection with Communism. And Pontecorvo thought Fuchs 'a highbrow'.)

In the summer of 1950 the family left for an Italian holiday. It was a happy-go-lucky affair: they camped by night, and took seven days to reach Italy. They called on Bruno's parents in Milan, and arranged to meet them a little later. Then they went on to Circeo, a holiday village near Anzio, south of Rome. There they were joined by other members of the family.

It was a very ordinary, carefree holiday. But then, on August 22nd, the Communist brother Gilberto arrived.

Then, on October 20th, 1950, the Rome newspapers

carried a startling story. British officials were trying to trace an Italian-born scientist who had disappeared! Until that moment few people in Britain or America had ever heard of Doctor Bruno Pontecorvo. True, a little earlier they had never heard of Doctor Klaus Fuchs.

As a naturalized British subject, Pontecorvo enjoyed full freedom of movement. If he wanted to go to Russia there was no legal method of preventing him. The fact that his flight was cumbered with cloak-and-dagger methods suggests Russian organization.

Certainly he himself had given no hint of his prospective move. On the contrary, he had just accepted a professorship at Liverpool University, and had taken a flat in the city.

On August 31st Pontecorvo and his family flew quite openly from Rome to Stockholm. Two days later they went on to Helsinki, in Finland—where they stayed in an apartment owned by the Soviet Embassy. Thence they were secretly smuggled into Russia: a Soviet ship, the *Bellastrov*, delayed its sailing from Helsinki to pick them up.

Now, and far too late, serious inquiries were made about Pontecorvo. One or two of his old acquaintances declared that he had always had Communist leanings—but others maintained that he was a dedicated scientist, completely uninterested in politics. Still, he had worked for three years in France under a famous Communist professor, and he had a Communist brother.

All these facts add up to very little. They should have prompted careful inquiry, but British screening authorities abhor Fascist methods. Nevertheless, the American F.B.I. learned of his family connections with Communism, however distant, by simply making inquiries of Pontecorvo's associates.

Some details of his journey to Russia were suggestive. At Rome he went to book seats to Stockholm; he produced Italian currency, but was told that as a foreigner he must pay in dollars. He returned a few hours later with the necessary 602 dollars. He wrote to his parents on the same day, regretting that he would not see them in Chamonix after all— and sent a postcard to Harwell promising to be back for a conference on September 7th. When the family landed at Stockholm they were within a few miles of Mrs Pontecorvo's parents, but they did not call or even telephone.

On his flight the more sensational newspapers assumed the worst. Here was another spy case akin to that of Doctor Fuchs. Such things, they declared, were bound to occur when Britain imported foreigners—though Doctor Alan Nunn May, the first of the atomic spies, was *not* a foreigner. By one report, Pontecorvo had been kidnapped. Or, while on his holiday at Lake Como, he had been contacted by a Czech and by an Italian, and later he had said, "I dare not go back to England. I should be sent to prison if I did." A good deal was made up of this story, but the Czech and the Italian were never identified; nor has anyone been found who actually heard the remark. And there was no reason at all why Pontecorvo should not have returned to Harwell, where he was in fact expected for a conference early in September.

So in popular imagination Pontecorvo was branded as a Russian spy: rumour does not need evidence. He was, it was assessed, a Communist who had long been in Russian employ. His masters were angry when he threw up his Harwell job to transfer to Liverpool, so they ordered him to Russia to augment their own nuclear staff. (Here the Pontecorvo story obviously borrows from that of Fuchs.) He had constantly handed over British atomic secrets to Russia.

Such was the current theory; but the 'evidence' supporting it would not have convicted a cat.

But another viewpoint was much simpler. Pontecorvo was flung by fate into France, the U.S.A., Canada, and England. His roots anywhere were feeble, and his national loyalties weak. He regarded himself as a professional scientist, belonging to no particular country.

Now Britain has never paid her outstanding servants adequately: Pontecorvo's salary was only a fraction of that of a pop singer. So the Russian approach was easy. They, like every other country, needed nuclear scientists: they simply offered Pontecorvo twice as much as he was getting in England. His subsequent roundabout journey was standard Russian conspiratorial practice.

He had not been a spy. His knowledge of nuclear weapons was well out of date, and the Russians knew them already from other sources. For more than two years he had been working on cosmic rays. True, he took with him to Russia a first-class brain and a large experience of nuclear research, but there is no jot of evidence that he ever spied for the Soviet Union.

However, an American Congressional report numbers him among the Soviet atomic spies. Pontecorvo himself declared in Moscow in 1955 that he had left the "capitalist world" because he could not stomach "the preparations being made for the use of atomic energy for military purposes". But he was not employed in such a task. The simple truth is that he was offered and accepted a better paid job.

II

There is a tendency in the West to distrust every word uttered in Russia—just as in Russia they are suspicious of any word uttered in the West. But is it not possible that Pontecorvo was speaking the truth when he said that he did not wish to be associated with nuclear weapons? Everything in his career supported this supposition. There was never a tittle of evidence to suggest that he had been a spy, or even a Communist—moreover, it does not follow that a Communist is necessarily a spy. As armaments are based on strong nationalist feelings, he would at least be lukewarm in his support of them, as he was virtually a man of no country whatever. His career since his defection to Russia is in keeping with his protest.

At first he was employed on the search for atomic materials. He had a laboratory at Kamenice, near the Czech uranium mines. Then he was reported to be in the Altai Mountains of Russian Siberia, a supply centre for thorium.

But in 1953 Western scientists established the European Organization for Nuclear Research (called CERN, after its French initials), with headquarters at Meyrin, near Geneva, Switzerland. Its aim was to pool ideas for non-militant nuclear research.

Three years later the Russians established their counterpart to CERN at Dubno, on the Volga, 90 miles north-east of Moscow. It was called the Joint Nuclear Research Institute, and its staff was drawn from all the Communist states—including China. Its director was the well-known Professor Blokhintsev, and one of the first appointments to his staff, in September 1956, was that of Dr Bruno Pontecorvo. Its purpose was "theoretical and experimental research in the field of nuclear physics".

The reader should note that both CERN and Dubno are pledged to study the *peaceful* uses of nuclear energy. Pontecorvo is known to have been intimately concerned in the objective of the establishment—he may even have suggested it.

Dubno is very well equipped: the Russians never begrudge money to scientific research. The initial expenditure was £45,000,000; the equipment included the world's most powerful atomic accelerator, a thousand million electron-volt proton synchronator. Far more was spent in the succeeding years.

What was a tiny village has become a town of 7000 inhabitants. The staff of the Institute numbers 2000, including 300 scientists. Russia supplies most of these, but there are also representatives from eleven other Communist countries—Albania, Bulgaria, China, Czechoslovakia, East Germany, Hungary, Outer Mongolia, North Korea, North Vietnam, Poland, and Rumania. (Yugoslavia is *not* included: indeed, it is represented in CERN.) Russia paid 47.25 per cent of the cost, China 20 per cent, and the smaller countries the rest. The contributions, both in cash and service, of some of these is trivial.

Pontecorvo has worked quite openly for Dubno since its foundation. The Institute has not been secret. It is in informal contact with CERN and with more than a hundred other nuclear organizations in the Western world.

When Mr Harold Macmillan visited Russia in March 1959 he was taken to Dubno—and Pontecorvo was one of the reception committee. The cynic might object that Mr Macmillan saw only what his hosts wanted him to see, and it is true that he is no nuclear scientist. But Dubno has also had visits from men like Sir John Cockcroft and Professor P. M. S. Blackett, and it would be *very* difficult to deceive them!

Doctor Pontecorvo is the chairman of the Scientists' Club

at Dubno, and a member of the Soviet Academy of Sciences —by this time he had become a Soviet citizen. In April 1963 he was awarded a Lenin prize of 7500 roubles (about £3000) for "research into the physics of neutrons and the weak interactions between elementary particles". He was described in the Russian Press as "one of the outstanding physicists of our time".

But there was an even more intriguing episode in November 1961. A number of the younger CERN scientists drafted a petition to all the nuclear powers calling for a suspension of testing of nuclear weapons. A copy was sent to Dubno: Pontecorvo promptly signed it, and persuaded several of his colleagues to follow his example.

All this surely suggests that the man was indeed sincere when he decided not to work on the production of nuclear weapons—though he had not actually done so since his transfer to Harwell, and would not have done so in Liverpool University. It will be noted that his apologia in 1955 blamed the "capitalistic world", not Britain in particular.

Alan Moorehead, in his interesting book *The Traitors*, summarizes a popular theory: that Pontecorvo had long been a Russian spy. During the War many people regarded Russia sympathetically. Maybe the Russians pressed money on him and got a receipt. But when he decided to leave Harwell for Liverpool he would have been useless as an agent. The Russians needed nuclear physicists, however, so ordered him to Moscow. If he had refused they would have denounced him to the British.

Mr Moorehead agrees that this is no more than surmise, and that there is not a scrap of evidence to support it.

Much more likely is another theory. Pontecorvo never was a spy; but at Harwell he was apprehensive because of his family background—its association with Communism. He imagined suspicion which did not exist. So he was easy prey for Russian agents, but did not finally make up his mind until his brother Gilberto met him in Italy. The terms offered by the Russians were excellent, both financially and professionally. His roots were not deep: to him one country was as good as another.

There is everything to suggest that his decision was then made abruptly. He had abandoned bank balances of £700 in England—and the heavy clothing he would need in Russia.

At the time of his flight exhaustive inquiries were made—he might have had accomplices. Nothing was unearthed which even suggested espionage; the only 'evidence' was his Communist brother. Pontecorvo was a defector, but no spy.

At first the Russians treated him with reserve—indeed, in 1951 there was a report that he had been arrested as a *British* spy! This was not confirmed. Today, obviously, he has been accepted as a loyal and valuable Soviet citizen.

SEVEN

The Lady Doctor

I

A BADLY WOUNDED BELGIAN OFFICER was wheeled
into the operating theatre of an improvised military hospital
near Fresnes, France, in 1916. The French were desperately
short of doctors, and had enlisted some women surgeons to
fill up the ranks. One of them was now 'scrubbing up' ready
for an operation.

The anæsthetist moved his cumbersome apparatus towards the table. His movements aroused the patient, who
opened his eyes. When they fell on the surgeon they betrayed
utter astonishment: he endeavoured to sit up, but failed. Yet
he did manage to speak: "That woman! Arrest her—she's
a German spy!"

The nurses attempted to soothe him: hallucinations are
common after a serious wound. But the man continued to
shout, until a preliminary whiff of chloroform quieted him.
The anæsthetist completed his preparations: now the patient
was ready for the surgeon. But she had disappeared. Nor
could any further trace of her be found.

Years later, on February 23rd, 1934, the Zürich

correspondent of the *Daily Express* reported the death from
tuberculosis, in a near-by sanatorium, of Madame Anna
Maria Lesser. Three days later the *Sunday Express* confirmed
the announcement, and added interesting details supplied by
the doctor in charge of her case. On her deathbed Madame
Lesser had confessed that she was a German, and had acted
as a German spy. She was, in fact, the famous Lady Doctor
whose identity had puzzled Allied Intelligence officers for so
long. The French newspapers were far more exuberant.

French Intelligence officers had known even before the
War that the Germans had a clever woman spy. It was they
who had christened her Mademoiselle Docteur. The Russians had another name for her, not nearly so polite. The
British identified her at different times as Bertha Heinrichsen,
Martha Scragmüller, Frau Köhr and Fräulein Janssen. The
newspapers preferred titles like "Red Tiger", "Tiger Eyes",
"the Black Cat", and "the Queen of Spies". Several writers
declared that she had been the spy-chief of Mata Hari.
At least one wrote a full-length biography of Madame Lesser,
who, it seemed, was more loquacious than is usual with retired
agents.

She *was* German. When she was young, pretty, and charming she became the mistress of Captain Karl von Wynanky.
He was a capable officer, but was always in debt—he had a
passion for gambling. At last the time came when the burden
of his debts became intolerable. He would have to leave the
Army—but some astute person had realized that he had
excellent qualifications for Intelligence work.

He was ordered to report to an insignificant office in
Berlin. The name of the firm was Meunier & Co.: it supplied
ball-bearings, tyres, and spare parts for motors—before the
First World War the motor trade was scarcely out of its

infancy; so the business was not large. However, its manager, an elderly man named Matthesius, was far-sighted, and had agents in the principal cities of Germany, France, Holland, and Belgium.

Von Wynanky, who spoke French fluently, was sent to Namur to establish a branch agency. He took Anna with him: his task involved a lot of entertaining, and an attractive 'wife' was a distinct asset. But at last Anna perceived that his work was not confined to the supply of ball-bearings and tyres. She was not in the least concerned: indeed, she volunteered to help.

She had some little skill as an amateur artist. When von .Wynanky gathered information about the forts of Namur he wrote his notes on a piece of canvas, and Anna painted a picture over them. In Berlin the paint was easily removed.

After some months the pair were to return to Berlin for a holiday—and further instructions. During the journey, however, von Wynanky was taken ill. There was a doctor on the train, and he diagnosed acute appendicitis. Karl was taken off the train at Cologne for an immediate operation, but he died during its progress.

Heartbroken though Anna was, she went on to Berlin and reported on her lover's work to Matthesius, who was amazed at her grasp of military details. Now, her task completed, she contemplated suicide, but he persuaded her to continue her lover's work.

She agreed, and flung herself enthusiastically into the training essential to such work. Her English was good and her French very good. She proved to be an apt student of military details, especially of armaments. And, as romance had died with her lover, nothing seemed to matter. She was very attractive, and ready to give her body as well as her brains to the service of her country.

Yet her first results were obtained by acute observation. The forts of Liège were strong, but the gaps between them were wide. Forces could easily pass between them while the forts were still in Belgian hands; but once the city was occupied, then the forts must soon surrender.

The officer who received her report insisted on seeing its author, to get further details—and was astonished to find that it was a woman. He was Colonel Erich von Ludendorff, who when war came laid the foundation of his reputation by using the very plan which Anna had suggested.

Her next assignment was in Lorraine, where she passed as a Swiss schoolmistress on holiday. There she became the mistress of an artillery officer, and by traditional pillow diplomacy extracted information from him. It was not very important, for the Germans were already well informed about French artillery tactics. But Anna's ingenious method of rounding off the episode without arousing any possibility of suspicion is worthy of mention. When she had exhausted her lover's knowledge she sent an anonymous letter to his wife; the aggrieved lady rushed to Lorraine and sent her husband's tearful mistress packing.

She kept to the same disguise during her visit to England in 1911. But for once Matthesius had blundered. Her training had been military, and the questions she asked at Cowes were so ingenuous that suspicion was aroused—and Anna made a hurried return to Germany.

Anna's methods were those of Delilah and Mata Hari, except that she had no access to well-known men. Her moral sense had died with her lover; her body could be used in the service wherein he had laboured.

She had one moment of serious danger. She concentrated on technical officers who might have detailed information to impart; only a few months before the War began in 1914 she became the mistress of a Belgian Engineer officer, Captain René Austin. One day they were out in a car; her handbag flew open, and pieces of paper blew out. She protested that they did not matter, but her lover insisted on recovering them.

He drove on, but Anna's intuition warned her—Austin had seen the notes she had made on one of the pieces of paper. He was her lover, but he was first and foremost a Belgian officer. At the next town he stopped and got out— to find a policeman? Anna drove on, and escaped.

But the hunt would be up. A casual incident led her to adopt an ancient device. Out in the country she ran over a pig, and killed it. Now was a chance to gain a few precious hours. She dragged the carcass of the pig into the driving-seat, stuck a hatpin through its ear, and set the car alight. Of course, detailed examination would reveal that the body was that of a pig; but whoever first found the car would see a blackened corpse inside it, and would not be tempted to closer acquaintance.

She did gain a few hours. She dropped a glove by the car, and made her way across country.[1]

This dramatic episode terminated Anna's career abroad, but when the War began she was transferred to counter-espionage. At this stage her history becomes confused, depending upon the imagination of the many authors who wrote it. An ex-inspector of the Special Branch of Scotland Yard wrote: "I recall seeing her on two occasions, in 1912

[1] I have mentioned that this subterfuge was not original. A lengthy account of Anna's exploit is given in *Die Weltkriegspionage*, a German book claiming semi-official status.

and 1914. She was an exceptionally beautiful creature. Further, she was clever and charming. Altogether, the type of woman who could fetch a man down like a punch from a boxing-glove with a horseshoe in it." Apparently when the War began she was sent to the Russian front, where she was recognized by a Russian Intelligence officer as a German spy he had seen in Vienna in 1908. "She was arrested, and shot as a spy. Her beautiful body was still warm as the victorious German cavalry galloped into the town, just twenty minutes too late to save the life of one of the cleverest women spies who had served in the ranks of their Secret Service."

However, she must have made a remarkable recovery from her 'execution'. A few weeks later she was active behind the German lines in France.

Yet she scored her greatest success in England. Not only did she learn about the new British implements of war later known as the tanks, she was actually present at their official trials. On her return to Germany her sketches and notes were passed to a colonel of Engineers for evaluation. His report on the new 'land-ship' was concise: the thing was impossible. No engine ever made could propel such a vehicle against such gradients.

(He was not the only doubter. Long after the War was over old files in the British War Office were being cleared out. In one was a design submitted by a Nottingham plumber in 1910: it bore a remarkable resemblance to the tanks of 1916. And a staff officer had scrawled across it: "The man's mad!" And, of course, H. G. Wells's vision in "The Land Ironclads" was treated as fantasy.)

When the 'land-ships' did eventually waddle across the Somme battlefield in September 1916 Anna sent a copy of the official report to the Engineer colonel. His honour and reputation impugned, he shot himself.

Yet Anna's active career was nearing its end. She was sent on a mission to France, and adopted her favourite 'disguise' —that of a woman doctor. It was on this mission that she had her narrow escape when a Belgian officer recognized her. No wonder he was startled to see her—he was Captain René Austin, who had once been her lover!

But, the discerning reader will protest, all this reads like imaginative fiction!

And he would be just about right.

II

The woman named Anna Maria Lesser did exist. She died in Switzerland in 1934, and on her deathbed she did claim to be the famous Lady Doctor, for whom British and French Intelligence officers had searched in vain during the War. But her claim was either an hallucination or a lie. Anna Maria Lesser had been a minor German agent. A good many stock stories had attached themselves to her—or, more likely, she herself attached them. She even applied to herself part of the Mata Hari legend. But the greater part of her claims were sheer fiction. She never went to England, much less saw the tank trials. She was not a doctor, and had no medical knowledge of any kind. Obviously she could not be shot dead in Russia and subsequently spy in France and England—actually she did neither. And Captain René Austin did not exist.

Yet there *had* been a German agent who was nicknamed the Lady Doctor. Some of her spies had been captured and persuaded to talk about her. They could not reveal her name because they never knew it.

H

There is far more authoritative confirmation that the
Lady Doctor did exist. Colonel Walther Nicolai was the
chief of the German Secret Service during the War. In 1924
he published a revealing book. In it he said: "It is remarkable
that it was an unusually well-educated woman who knew
best how to deal with the agents, even the most difficult and
crafty of them." Interrogated by German journalists, he
admitted that this woman was indeed known as the Lady
Doctor, but declined further details.

I was deeply interested in the woman. From time to time
I got hints as to her identity. I met a Dutch woman who
had been to school with her; now I was convinced that I had
the right name. But the Dutch lady's account contradicted
all the popular reports of the Lady Doctor as a "beautiful
woman spy". A photograph she produced demonstrated
that! But she certainly seemed to have a first-class brain.

With her identity known, my inquiries were more definite.
At last, in the summer of 1954, I walked into a house in a
quiet street in Munich. There lived Frau Claire Scragmüller,
and within a few minutes I knew that my trail had come to
its end. The Lady Doctor was dead, but her sister Frau
Scragmüller was still alive. Now I could write the full and
true story.

III

Elsbeth Scragmüller was born in 1888 at Mengede, a
Westphalian village near Dortmund. Her father was rural
burgomaster. The girl showed early promise in the local
schools, and passed on to Freiburg University. After taking
her degree she stayed on for postgraduate study. Her speciality was political economy, and she wrote a learned thesis on
the old Teutonic Guilds. For this she was granted her

doctorate—*not in medicine, but in philosophy.* "She never had the slightest interest in medicine, and scarcely knew how to bandage a cut finger." Captain René Austin, had he existed, would have had an uncomfortable time if she *had* operated on him!

One detail amused me. At a time when the British Secret Service was expending much time, effort, and money in seeking to know more of the Lady Doctor a copy of her philosophical thesis was in the British Museum Library!

When the War began in 1914 she was seized by the intense patriotism which then pervaded the countries involved. She wanted to do something for Germany. She had no interest in nursing. She would become a dispatch-rider, she decided—she even designed a uniform for herself.

The German army in those days was essentially masculine. A woman dispatch-rider—what nonsense! But in a train she met by accident Major Kefer, an officer of the German counter-spy service. Impressed by her intelligence, he gave her a post in the civilian censorship office at Brussels. It was not as romantic as dispatch-riding, but at least she was doing something.

She took her work very seriously. She began to tabulate the items of information she extracted from the letters she censored, and at last put them together in the form of a report. This attracted the attention of General von Beseler.

"Who is this man?" he asked of Major Kefer. "Obviously he has initiative—this report is very valuable. Who is he?"

Kefer had a sense of humour. "I'll send the author of the report to see you," he said. And the general got a real surprise when a girl walked into his room.

He was astonished at her grasp of military affairs, and had her appointed to the Special Intelligence Office at Antwerp.

There she was employed on the interrogation of suspected
spies. She did more than get incriminating information from
them—or from such as were really spies: she drew interesting
details about conditions in their own countries. At length the
brilliance of her work came to the notice of Colonel Nicolai,
head of the German Secret Service. He too was amazed to
find that his clever subordinate was a woman.

An Intelligence chief does not have to follow formal or
conventional lines. Elsbeth was commissioned as a lieutenant—then the only woman officer in the German Army.
She was posted to the Kriegnachrichtenstche at Antwerp—
the Office of War Information—first taking a special course of
espionage.

She was *not* trained as a spy: she *never* did any spying.
She did not have the face, figure, or temperament for the
traditional approach of the seductress spy: she remained a
virgin. But her active brain soon mastered the mysteries of
codes and ciphers, and she began to invent her own—some
were very ingenious.

A spy's weakest links are along his lines of communications,
the greatest difficulty often being not to get his information,
but to get it safely home. Thinking out innocuous methods
was one of Elsbeth's special tasks.

One of her agents, sent to England, carried a stamp album.
He was to pose as a keen collector, and was to exchange
stamps with a fellow-enthusiast in Holland. Stamps of
agreed countries represented different categories of warships
in harbour on the date of the postmark of the covering letter.

This was ingenious: it was scarcely Elsbeth's fault that
the man panicked as soon as he reached England, and gave
himself up!

Two other spies went to Portsmouth: their disguise was

that of cigar merchants, representing a Rotterdam firm. If they cabled an order for 3000 Coronas and 8000 Havanas, that meant that three battleships and eight cruisers were in port on the day. But the two agents were much too enthusiastic: in the course of a few days they ordered enough cigars to keep Portsmouth supplied for years—a detail which did not escape the notice of the censor. So Janssen and Roos died at the Tower of London.

The commandant at the spy school at Antwerp was Captain Heinrichsen; Elsbeth was one of the tutors. So when a British Intelligence officer identified her as Frau Captain Heinrichsen he was not too far off the mark.

The captured spies gave varying descriptions of their spy tutor. Joseph Marks, the stamp collector, declared that "Doctor Elsbeth" was called "Tiger Eyes" and terrorized her pupils. But prisoners invariably exaggerate. The fact was that the spy recruits were in general a poor lot. Many were released from gaols if they would 'volunteer' to spy. Others were riff-raff, anxious for easy money. Obviously the spy school had to impose a very strict discipline: this may be the basis of the 'terrorism' of which her pupils complained.

One item was common to all reports: Doctor Elsbeth was a drug addict. This perhaps accounted for her sudden rages, especially when her plans came to nothing: she hated failure.

She was reputed to have invented the 'fool-spy'. When an agent had failed, or had finished his usefulness, and she wished to be rid of him, she would send him on a mission on which he was certain to be caught. This is sheer fiction. It is true that an inordinate proportion of her pupils failed in their tasks, but that was due to circumstances for which Elsbeth was not responsible.

The spy school had been established in a building on a

corner of the Rue de la Pepinière in Antwerp—before Elsbeth joined its staff. Neither she nor her spy chiefs suspected that sharp-eyed Belgians had soon noticed peculiar activities going on in it, and that the British Secret Service had identified the building as a spy school.

Thereafter a constant watch was maintained by Belgian civilians—postmen and roadmen, maids in the houses opposite, even schoolboys playing marbles in the street. At first they supplied descriptions of the visitors who entered the house. Then they were supplied with ingenious cameras resembling wrist-watches. Thereafter visitors to the house were photographed. Thus, when the spies went into action, counter-spies in Britain and France were well prepared to receive them!

Rather late in the day the Germans got suspicious—so many of their agents were arrested very early in their mission. They took every precaution, but never knew how their spy school was kept under observation. It was, in fact, sheer folly to establish a spy school in a hostile city.

Doctor Elsbeth Scragmüller was kept busy. Apart from her task as a spy tutor, she continued to examine suspected spies and prisoners of war, and to check reports from spies working abroad—which were frequently imaginative! But she had *no* dramatic adventures. Belgium was the only foreign country she ever visited. Instead of the fantastic career attributed to her by journalists she merely did a good, sound job for her country. She gained high praise in official reports, and at the end of the War she was granted a military pension.

"She was not a bit like the descriptions of her printed in the books," said her sister. " 'The beautiful blonde beast', one author called her. She was blonde, but she had a homely, friendly face and a clear complexion. See, here are photographs of her.

"At Antwerp she did not get enough exercise, so she got too fat. But her brain was as active as ever. After the War she obtained a post as tutor in political economy at Freiburg University. Then she moved on to Munich. I cannot imagine why she remained a mystery for so long, as she lectured on her war experiences to the German Officers' Bund and Women's League—and these lectures were reported in the newspapers.

"But then she fell ill—consumption of the spine. She had an operation—a fragment of the spine was removed, and replaced with a piece of bone from her leg. But she was almost a cripple—she had to wear a steel corset. She could only manage to hobble about, all doubled up. You would have said that she looked a hundred.

"I nursed her. She often talked about her life in wartime— your synopsis is quite accurate. She never was a spy, and could never understand how such yarns began. All her 'adventures' concerned problems not of the body but of the mind.

"Our brother Johann did have adventures, but of a different kind. He had joined the Nazis, and became Chief of Police of Magdeburg. But he took his work too seriously— if Nazis broke the law he arrested them, and put them on trial as if they had been ordinary thugs. That made him unpopular in the Party. Further, he knew too much about the Reichstag fire—and he was bold enough to threaten Himmler. So he was one of those murdered on June 30th, 1934— 'the night of the long knives'.

"Elsbeth's illness was long and painful. In its last stages the doctors kept her constantly under sedatives—maybe that is the basis of the legend that she was a drug addict. She died in February 1940.

"I am sorry that I cannot show you her papers. On the morning of her death the police came—how they got to know I just can't imagine. They searched her desk and seized all her papers and took them away.

"At the moment I couldn't bother about such things. My aged mother was critically ill, and I had the air raids to bother me—and the struggle to get enough food. Anyway, I could not have defied the police, could I?"

So documentary information is not forthcoming. However, Frau Scragmüller's memory is clear and confident. Her sister was the Lady Doctor—of Philosophy: she worked in counter-espionage and spy-training, and was very competent in both. But she never saw a tank until after the War; nor did she seduce French officers. What is more, she never operated on anyone. She was never a 'Lady Doctor' in the medical sense—nor was she ever a spy.

EIGHT

Rutland of Jutland

I

MANY OF THE OFFICIAL SECRETS of the Second World War have been revealed and explained. But there has been no official comment on the events behind the strange and tragic story of Squadron-Leader Frederick J. Rutland, D.S.C., R.N.

Was this brilliant and heroic officer of the Royal Navy a Japanese spy? Or did some unknown officer of British Naval Intelligence make a dreadful mistake? The known facts suggest the latter probability.

Rutland was born in October 1886 at Weymouth, where as a small boy he watched great ships of the British Navy proudly riding at anchor in Portland Harbour. It is not surprising that his ambition was to become a naval officer, but his parents had neither the money nor the influence to obtain him a commission. So early in 1901 he joined the Navy as a boy.

He became an efficient seaman, and in his spare time studied the subjects necessary for what was in those days the rare achievement of promotion from the lower deck to the upper deck. He was much more the man of action than the scholar, but after twelve years he received His Majesty's commission in 1913. It is a tribute to this young officer that among still younger officers of a higher social class—which mattered a good deal in those days—he became widely respected for his efficiency, his initiative, and his gifts of leadership.

He volunteered for the Royal Naval Air Service—forerunner of today's Fleet Air Arm—had ten hours' flying at the Eastchurch flying school on the primitive wood-wire-and-canvas machines of the day, and qualified as a pilot.

Half a century ago it could be a hazardous enough operation to fly an aeroplane from and back to an airstrip on dry land. How much more dangerous it must have been to fly a seaplane from the deck of an early aircraft carrier, and then bring it down on the sea, to be recovered and hoisted back aboard. Rutland was a pioneer of such operations, as a result of which experience he submitted suggestions for carrier design that influenced the building of such vessels which were still in use over twenty years later. He insisted on trying out all dangerous innovations himself, and eventually succeeded in reducing his take-off run to as little as twenty feet!

He made naval history at the beginning of the battle of Jutland, when he took off in bad weather, spotted approaching enemy warships, and radioed their position back to his admiral. It was the first such achievement in the history of naval warfare, and for this he was awarded the Distinguished Service Cross and promoted to Flight-Commander.

Next day, during the battle, his ship, H.M.S. *Engadine*, went alongside the badly damaged and sinking H.M.S. *Warrior* to take off casualties. In a heavy swell their hulls were grinding together as stretchers were passed across from the doomed ship, and the last man slipped off his stretcher as the ships swung a few feet apart. At once Rutland seized the end of a coil of rope and dropped down between the ships, at the risk of being crushed to pulp at any moment. Holding on to the rope and to the bleeding and unconscious seaman, he was hoisted safely back aboard. For this act of "extreme and heroic daring" in saving life at sea he was awarded the Albert Medal First Class (in gold)—the only naval officer ever to survive to wear this decoration for an act of cold-blooded and suicidal heroism.

There is surely no need to give further details of this brave, brilliant, and patriotic officer. Sufficient has been told to indicate the type of man he was. It is difficult to imagine anyone less likely to act as a spy against his own country.

II

The strange story of Frederick Rutland can be divided into three periods: Glory, Mystery, and Tragedy. The period of Glory ended and that of Mystery began when in 1923, with the rank of Squadron-Leader, he suddenly resigned the commission he had worked so long and so hard to obtain. It is the first of several apparently contradictory acts in his life. He was thirty-seven years old, with an assured future in his service career, but with no experience that would have seemed to be of much use in civilian life. And Britain then had two million men seeking work.

A theory that Rutland was getting a divorce from his first wife and wished to remarry and start a new life seems hardly adequate to justify abandoning a promising career, unless there were other considerations that have never been revealed. But he did get his divorce, he did remarry, and shortly afterwards he took his new wife to Japan.

The views on the Japanese of modern readers are naturally
coloured by the well-authenticated stories of their atrocities
against helpless prisoners of war. These were inexcusable,
but, to some extent, understandable. Death does not seem
to mean much to the Japanese, and the ghastly form of suicide they call hara-kiri is accepted as a proper and creditable
way of registering a protest. Japanese soldiers who are taken
prisoner are regarded as morally dead, have been refused re-
entry to their country, and even ostracized by their families.
Japanese prison-camp officers to whom British prisoners
made protests against barbarous treatment have replied:
"You should not be here at all. If you had been Japanese you
would have died fighting for your country."

But though Japan had long been an ally of Britain, British
soldiers had never fought side by side with Japanese.
British Services had co-operated with Japanese only at sea
during the First World War, and the British-trained Japanese Navy had ways and traditions very different from those
of the German-trained Japanese Army.

When, after the First World War, Japan wished to re-
organize and modernize her naval air service the British
Government sent a technical commission to Tokyo headed
by the Master of Sempill, late of the Royal Naval Air Service.
So there was nothing in the slightest degree improper in
Rutland's accepting in 1923 an advisory post with the pro-
British Mitsubishi Aircraft Company, contractors to the
Japanese Admiralty and already employing a number of
other British aircraft experts.

Rutland now began to live a very different sort of life, with
a large house in the best part of Yokohama and a big, expensive car, which he drove with great skill but at a speed
which was apt to terrify his passengers. A powerful radio-set

was installed in his attic, and he had a remarkable range of elaborate photographic equipment. There was nothing secret about all this. In those days wireless telephony was a novelty to most people, and Rutland delighted in switching the set on to entertain visitors.

It was then that the legend of "Rutland the Mystery Man" began. He seemed to have unrestricted access to the secrets of Japan's naval dockyards, which was unusual, and permission to use his camera in those places, which was more unusual still. He spent much time in his dark-room, and more time busy with his big radio-set. These facts suggest that he was engaged on some sort of Intelligence work; and that he could have been working only against the Japanese.

But the Japanese had a quite efficient counter-espionage department of the Kempei-tai, and Rutland looked so obviously European that he could not have passed unrecognized among the Japanese seamen and dockyard workers. Had he, then, some highly placed Japanese official 'protection'? And, if so, in return for what secret services could such protection have been offered? Rumours spread that he was selling British naval secrets to the Japanese, but the whole history of the man makes such an idea seem ridiculous. And certainly his dark-room and radio-room could have had no part in passing to the Japanese the knowledge and experience stored away in his brain.

Early in 1927, while his family were away on holiday, his house was mysteriously burnt down. There was much gossip among the British community, and unkind rumours of arson. But the insurance money barely recouped Rutland for his losses, so the motive could not have been financial.

The fire, whether accidental or sinister, seems to have been the beginning of the end of Rutland's period of usefulness in

Japan. He left the country a few months later—and seems to have been very pleased to do so.

III

Back in England with his family, Rutland took up one of the few types of civilian job for which his personal charm and his wide experience of internal-combustion engines qualified him. He became a car salesman. He acquired a pleasant house in the Thames Valley, and lived in comfort, if not in obvious prosperity.

Then another mysterious thing occurred: while he and his family were away on holiday the Thames Valley house was burnt down! If the Yokohama fire had been intended to destroy evidence sought by the suspicious Kempei-tai that he was a British spy, could the Thames Valley fire have been intended to destroy evidence sought by a suspicious MI5 that he was a Japanese spy? Or was it just a strange coincidence that burned homes heralded the end of his period of residence in one country after another?

Whatever the reason, Rutland did not stay long in England after his second fire, and in 1937 he and his family moved to California. He started a business as an investment broker, not in so obvious a locality as New York's Wall Street, but in the business quarter of Los Angeles. He might have been expected to need some time to learn his new job, build up a connection, and, after a few years perhaps, to achieve modest prosperity. But Rutland appeared to be prosperous from the start, with a fine house at Beverley Hills, a private swimming-pool, and with his children educated at the best schools. Where did the money come from? If he had saved a large sum from his work as a car salesman, why did he not stay in England and continue with his work? Why on earth should he have gone thousands of miles away to start, as an alien, in a highly competitive business of which he knew nothing?

For any attempt to answer those questions we must enter the realm of speculation. We must first assume that Japanese naval successes in the Russo-Japanese War did not greatly surprise the far-seeing and well-informed British NID, the Naval Intelligence Department. But we must also assume that NID were later impressed by what the Japanese navy did in the First World War as an ally of Britain. In view of her vast interests in the Far East, Britain welcomed an ally, but she did not want a rival. It is an axiom of her strategic planning that as soon as Britain has won one war she begins to think of the next. And in the early nineteen-twenties it is highly probable that the Committee of Imperial Defence asked for a plan from the Admiralty, based on the assumption that in some future war the increasingly efficient Japanese Navy might be a threat to Britain's Far Eastern interests. And how right the Committee were was proved disastrously less than twenty years later. So, bearing in mind what had been learned during the First World War of the increasing importance of naval aircraft, the plain duty of NID was to find out all it could about Japanese naval air power. I am now suggesting that Rutland's record for courage and patriotism and technical efficiency led to his being asked in 1923 to resign his commission and go to Japan as a civilian and as a British spy. The suggestion is supported by the facts.

Rutland did his work for the Mitsubishi Company conscientiously and well. If he were working for NID, he served them equally well and conscientiously. How he obtained 'protection' from the Kempei-tai, if he did so, we may never know. The most brilliant spies are likely to arouse suspicion in time, and it may be that Rutland was warned in 1927 that the Kempei-tai were on his trail, with suspicion but with no proof. The proof lay in his home, with its photographic and radio equipment: with the burning of the house, all proof would be destroyed. Then he felt himself to be *persona non grata*, and went home to England. And there, with his mission accomplished and his reports filed in the archives of NID, he was 'retired' in the economical British way and left to fend for himself until he might be needed again.

While Rutland was wasting his talents and experience as a car salesman during the nineteen-thirties the Committee of Imperial Defence was becoming increasingly concerned at the aggressive policy of Japan. Japanese statesmen of moderate views were murdered by the killers of reactionary secret societies. We know now that the Anglo-Japanese alliance had caused Britain to lose face throughout the Far East, where the Japanese were distrusted and suspected of imperial ambitions. It was important to know how far, and how fast, Japan was slipping away from British influence.

The basic facts were ominous: they were based on the inescapable vital statistics of Japan. Between 1926 and 1936 the population of Japan had increased from 59,000,000 to 70,000,000, and was rising at the rate of 1,000,000 per annum. The problem was not one of politics but of survival. Britain opposed, but understood, Japan's hope of conquering enough Chinese territory to settle millions of surplus Japanese peasants.

By late 1936 the far-sighted men of the Committee of Imperial Defence in Whitehall knew that war with Hitler's Germany was practically inevitable. So what, they asked themselves, would be Britain's position in the Far East?

Could Britain rely on her aggressive Japanese ex-allies, who had imperial ambitions of their own? The shattering answer came on November 25th, 1936, when MI6 reported that Germany and Japan had signed the Anti-Comintern Pact. Exactly a week later the *Tokyo Asahi* said: "It would be too hasty for Japan to decide her foreign policy without examining first whether England is Japan's friend or her enemy."

So Britain had reached the strategic crossroads: Should she protect her Far Eastern possessions by remaining friendly with the only Power with the motive—or the ability—to attack them? If so, she would have had to remain neutral towards the Anti-Comintern Pact and let Hitler proceed with his plans to make all continental Europe part of the Third Reich. Or should Britain, implacably opposed to a German-dominated Europe, range herself against Germany and so, by implication, against Japan? If so, she would risk losing Singapore, risk Japanese invasion of restless India, risk Japanese invasion of weakly defended Australia— a possibility of which Australian statesmen were all too conscious.

December 1936 was a milestone in British Far Eastern foreign policy. When World War Two came, as seemed inevitable, what would Japan do? What, in fact, *could* Japan do? What chance did the British Pacific Fleet stand against the untested pilots and machines of the Japanese naval air force?

It did not take much research among NID records to establish the fact that the officer best qualified to answer those vital questions was Frederick Rutland.

It appears, then, that early in 1937 Rutland was, in Intelligence jargon, 're-activated' by NID, and was directed to set up a new British naval spy-ring working against Japan. He

I

knew the Japanese mentality, and still had friends and
contacts in the Mitsubishi Company. But he had reason to
believe that he was still on some ten-year-old Kempei-tai
suspect-list. Japanese counter-espionage was known to be
surprisingly poorly equipped technically—for instance, its
direction-finders for spy radios were hopelessly out of date—
but it had some competent spy-catchers among its officers.
Rutland would have been acting with proper caution if he
had decided to control his new spy-ring from the safety of
the nearest neutral territory, in the same way that the Resident Directors of the Russian Secret Service always directed
their networks in one country from a headquarters in an
adjoining country. China was in a too unsettled state to offer
a safe base. But a suitable, if distant, base from which
Rutland could carry on his work would be some big port on
the American Pacific seaboard, where couriers could be
recruited from among the crews of ships trading with Japan—
and from among the thousands of Japanese settled in Los
Angeles or San Francisco.

But the establishment of a safe base and lines of communication were merely operational details. The object of the
enterprise was to obtain secret information from inside Japan,
a country whose people are in general very patriotic and
therefore not susceptible to bribery in matters of national
security. Readers with a knowledge of Intelligence techniques will agree that Rutland's most hopeful line of approach
to Japan would have been as a double spy.

The double spy may be either a patriot or a traitor; but,
whichever he is, he treads a psychological tightrope which
only a determined character can successfully negotiate. The
fairly recent British case of George Blake is an example.
Basically, a double spy must start by being a genuine spy for

nation A. He then approaches nation B and offers, for a price, to doublecross nation A. Nation B welcomes the chance to recruit a member of nation A's Intelligence service, and the double spy begins to draw two salaries. Then he reminds nation B that if he is to keep his position as a spy for nation A he must feed back some secret information. Nation B sees the force of this argument and supplies the spy with suitably 'doctored' material, welcoming the chance to deceive the enemy. All that is Intelligence routine.

The next stage of a double-spy operation is vitally important. If he is a traitor to nation A he usually does not much care what happens so long as the flow of easy money continues from two different sources. But if he is a patriot— and it is inconceivable that Rutland could have been other than a patriot-spy—he reports the full facts to nation A, to which he owes his primary loyalty. Intelligence evaluators of nation A then consider the information fed back to them, in the light of their knowledge from their spy that it has been doctored. And when you know what an enemy *wants* you to know you can make very shrewd guesses as to what he wants to *conceal*. It is not surprising, incidentally, that after many years of such twisted thinking Intelligence officers are apt to find themselves heading for the psychiatrist's couch!

Knowing the fanatically patriotic Japanese mentality as he did, Rutland would have realized that they would despise and distrust anyone who offered to betray his own country. But they would be prepared to accept his services if he were offering to betray a country to which he owed no natural loyalty. Had Rutland approached the Japanese and offered to betray Britain in return for cash and doctored information they would not have tolerated him. But if he had approached them from United States soil and offered to betray America, there is no reason why his offer should not have been accepted with alacrity. For Japanese Intelligence officers have always been hampered by the physical differences between East and West: Japanese patriot-spies are useless in Western countries, and recourse has to be made to Western traitors.

Hence the facts suggest that early in 1937 Rutland was (*a*) actually a spy for Britain against Japan; (*b*) pretending to the Japanese that he was working on secret naval projects for the United States; (*c*) offering to work for Japan as a double-spy against America in return for cash and doctored information; (*d*) reporting to NID in Whitehall; and (*e*) passing on to United States Naval Intelligence such material from Japanese sources as might interest them.

There is no doubt that Rutland was working as a Japanese agent—not necessarily the same thing as a spy. In a peacetime U.S.A. there are few inviolable secrets. An agent can obtain a large amount of useful information quite legally, from Government publications or technical magazines. Years ago I discussed this with Captain von Rintelen, who organized a German spy service in America during the First World War. He said that there was little which he could not buy—not from traitors, but from the Government Printing Office. His difficulty was, in fact, the superabundance of available information: the U.S.A. is a vast place, with widespread activities. Almost all of these were reported in the Press or in Government manuals, but the quantity and distribution would have needed hundreds of agents to pick out the information of direct use to their employers and to evaluate it. "I was swamped with paper," he said. "Any or every sheet could have been important, but it was physically impossible to sift it all."

So Rutland could satisfy his Japanese clients by purchasing and forwarding published information. As his association with American Naval Intelligence grew closer its officers would pass on to him items of unpublished information which they would like the Japanese to believe!

IV

When a spy is given a new assignment he must avoid suspicion by having a 'cover' occupation, such as Peter Kroger's cover as a dealer in antique books in the Portland spy case. For this purpose it is usual for a grant to be made from his country's secret service funds to establish him in his cover job. And this, incidentally, can be a sound investment: the man who was probably the most brilliant and successful spy in history, Dr Richard Sorge, set up his German radio operator in business as a radio dealer, and the profits from the business eventually covered the cost of the entire Soviet spy system in Japan!

So if Rutland drew from NID the cash to set himself up in business in Los Angeles, and if he also drew a similar sum from the Japanese, we have the explanation of the financial splash with which he set up his new and lavish home in exclusive Beverley Hills.

It was at that early Los Angeles stage that the seeds were sown of Rutland's tragic destiny. No country runs a single unified Intelligence service. There are certain practical difficulties which prevent this. Britain has her broadly interpreted Military Intelligence Department, MI5, which operates for counter-espionage purposes within the Commonwealth; She has MI6, commonly known as the Secret Service, which operates for direct espionage purposes outside the Commonwealth; she has NID, which is exclusively concerned with naval matters; and others.

Rutland's spy-outpost in Los Angeles was outside the direct supervision of any secret NID post in the United States. Hence it is probable that NID asked the world-wide organization of MI6 to check and report on Rutland. It would reveal that Rutland was apparently spending far more than his known income. In all Intelligence work it is vital to follow up any case in which a man is spending more money than he is known to be receiving. The activities of those convicted in the Portland spy case came to light through the lavish spending of the drunken fool Harry Houghton.

Hence in 1937 a report would appear on Rutland's file that he was living with suspicious extravagance; the last thing NID would have done would be to reveal the fact that Rutland was a double spy. He may have suffered sadly at the end from the very efforts that had been made to protect him.

Let us now return to the known facts. We must remember that Rutland was typically British, and unfamiliar with the American way of life. In a London West End club it is 'not done' to try to sell vacuum cleaners or whatever to fellow-members. He did not realize that Americans have different ideas. In his excellent biography, *Rutland of Jutland*, author Desmond Young quotes a letter from a Los Angeles friend of the Rutland family: "He [Rutland] made no secret of the fact that he had worked for a Japanese firm on the construction of naval aircraft. My recollection is that he made several trips back there on business. As for his ostensible occupation as an investment broker, I cannot recall that he ever tried to interest any of his friends or acquaintances in investments, which is unusual."

Another of those sets of initials now enters our story: USNI—United States Naval Intelligence—a department which had long and carefully watched Japanese naval activities in the Pacific. A key USNI listening-post was at San Diego under a famous Intelligence chief, Captain Ellis Zacharias, who used a cut-out to collect information about Rutland's activities from an English friend, Dr Dinsley. There is ample evidence that USNI knew more about what Rutland was doing than has ever been revealed.

All available evidence points to the fact that Rutland was supplying valuable information to the Americans, Dr Dinsley acting as cut-out man who carried the information to Captain Zacharias. It suggests that Rutland was doing a tricky job against the Japanese on behalf of British NID, and, having fulfilled his duty to his own country, was doing what he could to help her future American allies. In return for this he was kept off the USNI 'black list', and his movements remained unrestricted, which would certainly not have been the case unless high U.S. Intelligence authorities had been satisfied that his work for the Japanese was no more than a pretence in the interests of Britain and America.

It is an open secret now that Pearl Harbor was not quite such a surprise to U.S. Intelligence as was once generally believed. But that is another story, about which many books could be—and some have been—written. It would be surprising if Rutland had not known in advance of the Pearl Harbor attack. It would have been equally surprising if he had not known details of Japanese naval air power in the South Pacific, and the relatively feeble defences of the British Pacific Fleet against air attack. It seems probable that Rutland sent report after report on his secret radio transmitter to Whitehall, appealing for better air protection for Britain's

capital ships based on Singapore. Then he became desperate
at mere formal acknowledgments from Whitehall, and at last
he determined to leave his post and make a personal appeal
in London for some action which would help to protect a
vital outpost of the Empire he loved so deeply and had served
so well.

It is certain that during the last few days of November
1941 Rutland made a sudden, and fateful, decision. He
rushed to the airport of Los Angeles (unhindered, be it noted,
by American Intelligence authorities), flew in an American
aircraft to Montreal, and thence 'thumbed a lift' in a Royal
Air Force plane to England. And that was at a stage in the
War when R.A.F. Ferry Command did not lightly carry
unauthenticated civilians across the Atlantic!

In London, early in December, he made a statement to
the Admiralty. In the restrained words of Desmond Young's
book, Rutland "was given a complete brush-off. According
to his own story, the officer who saw him said, in effect,
'There's nothing you can tell us that we don't know already.
Good-day to you!' And then, on the morning of Sunday,
December 7th, came Pearl Harbor."

Rutland had flown back to England with warnings for the
Admiralty. American Naval Intelligence had, of course, been
watching Japanese fleet movements very carefully: Captain
Zacharias was only one of those who believed that a sudden
attack by carrier-borne aircraft was imminent.

Rutland did not know all the details, of course. But he
was as well informed as any man in the world about the
efficiency of the Japanese naval air service. Hence he went
to the Admiralty to warn them that the sudden strike at the
American Fleet was not merely feasible but imminent. He
had another warning to add: Churchill had announced the

arrival of the battleship *Prince of Wales* and the battle cruiser *Repulse* at Singapore. It was *not* announced, but was known in naval circles, that the aircraft-carrier which should have accompanied them had not in fact sailed. Rutland's most emphatic warning was desperately urgent: the capital ships at Singapore should never venture beyond the range of fighter-aircraft cover.

But, three days after the tragedy at Pearl Harbor, the two warships sailed from Singapore to oppose a Japanese landing in Malaya. When they were beyond air-cover limits they were attacked by a swarm of Japanese bombers. Both ships were sunk, with a loss of 800 men; and Malaya and Singapore were doomed. Two hours of air bombing had upset the whole basis of British war-time strategy in the Far East.

So what next happened to Rutland? Was he recalled to the Admiralty? Was he thanked, rather late in the day, for the information he had eagerly crossed half the world to offer? Was he tendered apologies for the fact that his warnings had been ignored, at great cost to Britain?

On December 16th, 1941, Rutland was arrested under Section 18b of the Defence Regulations, and locked up with a motley collection of potential spies and traitors in Brixton Prison.

V

It is more than a quarter-century now since the Defence Regulations of the Second World War came into force in liberty-loving Britain. Many of the regulations were a negation of the personal liberties which the British people had fought for since the days of Magna Carta. And the most controversial of all was Defence Regulation 18b, under which British subjects could be detained and held in custody not for anything they had *done*, but for what they *might* do. And what secret-service agent, what police-officer, what judge, what jury, could possibly have said definitely what was in a certain individual's mind at a certain point in time? Ethically, Regulation 18b was quite indefensible.

But in 1940 and 1941, when the Regulation was widely enforced, Britain was literally fighting for her life. No greater danger had threatened her shores since the Norman Conquest—not even the Spanish Armada or the invasion plans of Napoleon. In the practical British way the people agreed that they must surrender their liberties for today in order that they might ensure those liberties for tomorrow and for all time.

For a generation the patient and fair-minded officers of MI5 had been building up thousands of dossiers on individuals who hated their own country and were ready to help their country's enemies. And when the showdown came these suspects—and they were never more than suspects— were not shot out of hand, as they would have been in Russia; they were not sent to lingering death, the gas-chamber, and the incinerator, as they would have been in Nazi Germany: they were sent to spend the rest of the War in the peace and safety and comparative comfort of a hotel in the Isle of Man. If there had to be a Regulation 18b, let us at least agree that it was administered by fair-minded officers of the hand-picked Intelligence Service in the most humane possible way, checked with the greatest possible care by the Home Office Advisory Committee, under Norman Birkett, which reviewed every single case.

We need not waste any pity on those 18b detainees who

might have been guilty, but let us try to understand that those whom we may now know to have been innocent were interned for what appeared to be a good reason in those hectic days of the early nineteen-forties, when Britain was fighting for survival. Britain tried to play fair even with those who might have constituted a murderous Fifth Column.

Many of the arrests made in the urgency and emotion of the day were later proved to have been unjustified. Of the 1829 people arrested under Regulation 18b, 1603 were released long before the end of the War.

It is a pity that we shall never know what thoughts passed through the active brain of Frederick Rutland during the long days and weeks and months that he walked the Manx shores, and stared across from Douglas towards the island that was the beloved country he had tried his best to serve. He remained faithful to the traditions of secrecy of his department. Defence Regulation 18b was precautionary, not accusative. To members of his family Rutland would say, "If you're not accused you can't prove you are innocent." The Secret Service is—secret.

He had made one fatal error. When he hurried home from Los Angeles he went to the Operations Section of the Admiralty, which was most concerned with the imminent Japanese menace. But in this section he was unknown: had he gone to the Intelligence Department, where he had friends who would have listened to him with respect, the consequences would have been very different.

He was never charged. Naval friends like Admiral Sir Roger Keyes and Commander R. T. Bower, who were both Members of Parliament, constantly pressed the Home Secretary for information, but failed to elicit any meaningful word. True, on one occasion the Home Secretary did state

that "American Intelligence authorities blamed Rutland for
the Pearl Harbor disaster." But this was completely untrue.

The basis for Rutland's arrest was much simpler. Not
unnaturally, he was angry at his 'brush-off' in the Admiralty.
And, when a few days later the warning he had carried home
was proved so dramatically to be only too well justified, he
was heard to say, "If the Admiralty had listened to my
warning the *Prince of Wales* and *Repulse* would never have
been sunk." In those days, when espionage activity was
exaggerated a thousandfold by rumour, criticism of authority
could be classed as treason.

The Home Secretary referred more than once to Rutland's
"hostile associations". It was quite true that he had plenty
of Japanese naval friends; but this could surely have been
exploited for Intelligence purposes instead of being made a
basis for suspicion of treason.

Rutland was one of the 1603. He was released in September
1943 after less than two years of detention. There was no
charge, no trial, no explanation, no apology: and the War
was at its height. Sir Roger Keyes and Commander Bower
still fought for his honour. But mud sticks: Rutland had
been branded as a suspected spy, and the suspicion haunted
him for the rest of his life. Ten years after his death a highly
respected British newspaper published a sensational story
under the headline "Briton aided Pearl Harbor attack". It
was based on the old bogy that "American Intelligence
authorities" had made the assertion. The newspaper, when
its story was challenged, was correct enough to consult
Captain (now Rear-Admiral) Zacharias. If the yarn *had* been
true he would certainly have known! The newspaper published his disclaimer—but a denial never catches up with
the original rumour.

VI

After his release from internment Rutland went to live alone in a cottage at Beddgelert, in Caernarvonshire. His eldest son was a practising doctor. His wife and two younger children were American citizens in California. Rutland was not the sort of man who would let anyone suffer on account of his own problems.

Rutland's doctor son received a heartbreaking letter from his father on January 29th, 1949:

"You know my views on life and death. My life has been an adventurous one, always full of excitement. . . . I have always told myself that so long as life was worth the living I would live it to the full, and when it no longer held any real interest it would be time to go.

"I feel that time has now come. . . .

"Go down to Dorking. Take the Leith Hill road. About two miles out you will cross a stream. On the far side of the bridge you will find a footpath on the right. You will find me about thirty yards down this path amongst some bushes. . . ."

But Squadron-Leader Frederick Rutland did not die on a quiet Surrey footpath, where birds sang in the trees and a stream tinkled over stones. He died, during the night of January 28th, of gas poisoning in a bedroom of the Grosvenor Court Hotel in Davies Street, in London's noisy West End. To the coroner's verdict of "self-administered coal-gas poisoning" was added a rider to the effect that Rutland killed himself "while the balance of his mind was disturbed".

We cannot help wondering what report was made by that faceless Admiralty official who interviewed Rutland during those critical days of early December 1941; or what Admiralty

Registry bottleneck prevented certain Top Secret files from being connected with the report. Only the very highest officers of NID have access to the records of 'double spies'.

Perhaps the whole episode was the result of a regrettable clerical error.

'Regrettable' is the word.

NINE

Mass Murderer

I

DURING THE GERMAN OCCUPATION of Paris in the Second World War Doctor Petiot was accused of twenty-seven murders. But he boasted that he had committed over sixty!

When the Allied armies chased the Germans out of Paris he was in hiding. In those hysterical days immediately after the Liberation an even worse crime than murder was collaboration with the enemy. And French newspapers widely alleged that Doctor Petiot had been a German secret agent, and most people believed them.

There is no reasonable doubt that during the Occupation he was in touch with high officials of the Paris Gestapo. But now that, twenty years after, we can take a more objective view, the fact emerges that, instead of corrupt German officials paying Doctor Petiot for his services, he was paying *them*! He was always the lone wolf and unlikely to have been anybody's agent. We have only to set out the facts and let them speak for themselves.

A greater Frenchman than Petiot once said, "I don't ask

143

for brilliant generals—just lucky ones." Doctor Petiot was not a brilliant man, but he was certainly a lucky one.

Born in January 1897, Marcel-André-Henri-Félix Petiot had no proper and normal parental supervison during the critical years of adolescence. He was eight years old when his father died, and thirteen when his mother died, after which he was brought up by a well-meaning aunt. Even in his schooldays he was an anti-social type. At the age of sixteen he was caught robbing pillar-boxes. But, as that ambitious and rather likeable crook Horatio Bottomley said, when refusing to discharge an office boy caught fiddling with the postage book, "After all, we all have to start in a small way!"

In spite of that early record Petiot became a medical student. Conscripted and sent to the Western Front during the First World War, he was lucky enough to suffer a minor wound in the foot, which took him out of the trenches and relegated him to the comparative safety of a casualty clearing station. His medical studies, however incomplete, qualified him to administer pain-killing drugs to seriously wounded *poilus*, but he found it more profitable to let them scream with agony while he stole the morphia which would have relieved them, and peddled it in the Black Market. Neither a patriot nor a traitor, he was then, as throughout his life, merely an exponent of private enterprise, making a few francs at any cost in human suffering or human life.

For a series of such contemptible crimes he was court-martialled. A good stiff punishment might possibly have frightened him into reformation. But he was not punished at all—he was rewarded! He was given an expensive course of psychiatric treatment and a disability pension. He can hardly be blamed for laughing at his humanitarian judges and for feeling that Crime Often Pays.

Dismissed from the French Army, he completed his medical studies, qualified as a doctor, and in 1921 began to practise at Villeneuve-sur-Yonne. He seems to have been a reasonably capable doctor, and acceptable socially, and in due course he became mayor. There was some unkind gossip when his attractive housemaid became pregnant, but the girl disappeared and was never heard of again, and in time the gossip died down. It was undoubtedly his first experiment in murder, and was encouragingly successful.

Mayor Petiot married Georgette Lablais, and she bore him a son, but, despite his domestic happiness, his lifelong craving for money impelled him to risk everything for a few crooked francs. Among his patients was wealthy old Madame Debauve. She was found robbed and murdered, and a prominent local citizen had the effrontery to accuse his Worship the Mayor of the crime. It seemed an incredible charge. What is still more incredible is that the same prominent local citizen should have submitted himself to treatment for rheumatism by Doctor Petiot. The complaint is always painful but seldom fatal, but soon the patient died! An autopsy was ordered, and it was very convenient for Doctor Petiot that he should carry it out himself! It is hardly surprising that he reported finding no trace of poison in the body.

It seemed that rumours of these suspicious events in Villeneuve-sur-Yonne reached the authorities in Paris. Detectives of the Sûreté made investigations, and a bulky dossier was compiled. But later some friendly hand removed it from the files, and it disappeared for ever.

In more than one French murder trial there has been a suggestion of 'protection', or of 'adjustment' of evidence. There have even been cases in which State intervention has been suggested. Consider, for example, the strange story that

K

in 1922 Henri-Désiré Landru was not executed at all for his
many murders—of which, admittedly, the proof was insufficient—that he was smuggled to South America with a
Government pension, and that he was seen and recognized
there by the world-famous clown Grock, who relates the
incident in his autobiography. It would seem that long
before the Second World War Doctor Petiot was enjoying
some similar and sinister form of official 'protection'.

Then a series of petty local thefts began to worry the
police at Villeneuve-sur-Yonne. A trap was set, and the thief
was caught red-handed. It was the Mayor! He was tried and
found guilty, and sent to prison for three months. When he
was released—apparently with no blot on his professional
copybook—he shifted his home to Paris and put up his
brass plate outside No. 66 Rue Caumartin. By 1936 he was
in the hands of the police again, this time for robbing book-
shops. He was tried, found guilty, and discharged for further
psychiatric treatment.

Doctor Petiot had now been three times suspected of
murder; three times convicted of theft; twice adjudged on the
borderline of insanity. It would have saved the lives of scores of
decent French citizens if this evil creature had then been
locked up permanently in a prison or lunatic asylum. But all
that happened was that after his 'treatment' he was released,
still a fully qualified doctor, to continue his career of crime.

During the next few years there is evidence that he
committed further murders. But what he actually did may
seem to many to be something even worse than murder. He
peddled narcotics, which as a doctor he could so easily
obtain. It is a dreadful crime to destroy human life within
hours by poison. But it can be argued that an even worse
crime is to destroy human minds—souls, if you will—over a

period of years by encouraging and pandering to the craving of drug addicts, for the sake of a few francs. Cases are on record in which Doctor Petiot, when accused of such crimes, murdered his victim *and* his accuser, and yet again evaded retribution.

II

The Second World War came, and Doctor Petiot managed to avoid serving his country. Then the uneasy period of the 'phoney war' ended, and the French were defeated. Some formed the Resistance Movement, but Doctor Petiot preferred to make money out of his country's misfortunes.

After the German occupation of Paris, French Jews began to be rounded up in thousands for transfer to the Nazi extermination camps. Those who had neither money nor influence were gassed and incinerated. Those who had money cannot be blamed for trying to escape abroad—and they were just the types in whom Doctor Petiot began to take a great interest. He recruited a little gang of underworld touts, who passed round the whispered news that anyone who wanted to be smuggled out of France to sanctuary in a neutral country could be accommodated—at a price.

Nazi discipline was strict, but some of its leaders managed to evade it, to their own advantage. High-ranking Gestapo officials offered, for instance, to sell wealthy and influential Jewish prisoners to the Allies for cash. Even the notorious Adolf Eichmann was involved in a projected deal to exchange Jewish prisoners for military trucks. The indubitable fact is that officers of the Paris Gestapo were not merely ready but eager to accept bribes in return for allowing wealthy Jews to escape abroad. And Doctor Petiot similarly perceived opportunities of making a few more crooked francs.

So wealthy French Jews began to disappear from the streets of Paris. And nobody asked awkward questions. A friend of mine happened to be in the bar of an exclusive Paris club during the Occupation. An elderly and wealthy French Jewish bachelor came in with a beaming smile. "Tomorrow," he murmured to a friend, "I shall disappear. Nobody must make any inquiries about me. That might cost me my life. In a few days I shall be safe in Argentina, and I shall communicate with you. I may even be able to advise you how you can join me. But, in the meantime—not a word!"

And thereafter not a word was ever heard of him.

Until he had accumulated some capital from his dreadful trade Doctor Petiot had to take certain risks. Parts of bodies began to be found dumped in Parisian suburbs, dismembered in a way that indicated professional training and experience. But the money was flowing in very satisfactorily, and Doctor Petiot soon had enough to acquire special premises at No. 21 Rue Lesueur, a large house of which he used only two ground-floor rooms, and to which he had made some sinister adaptations. One was a small, sound-proof, windowless, triangular killing-room; another was an outsize 'inspection pit' in the garage. And already installed was a large furnace for the central heating system.

If we accept the number of people Doctor Petiot claimed to have murdered, then during the operating period of his new *abattoir* his victims must have been passing through it at the rate of about one every ten days. Hopeful escapees had two interviews with the apparently helpful doctor. One, and one only, lived to tell his story of what was said at the first interview. None ever survived to tell what happened at the second.

The prospective victim was brought to Rue Lesueur by

one of the touts, who was paid his generous fee and departed in search of another victim. It is not suggested that the touts knew the eventual fate of their clients; they genuinely thought they were helping innocent citizens to escape from the Gestapo and the German death-camps, and they cannot be blamed for requiring substantial fees for risking their own lives.

Having sworn his victim to secrecy, Doctor Petiot directed him to withdraw his bank balance, turn all his stocks and shares into cash, and bring cash, jewellery, and other valuables to Rue Lesueur at night on a certain date. He must then be ready for immediate departure with the nest-egg that he believed would help to establish himself in some unspecified neutral country. One of the earlier victims is known to have brought along two million francs in French currency and several thousand American dollars. Doctor Petiot's overheads were large, but his profits from between sixty and seventy such victims were enormous.

Exactly what happened at the second interview will never be known, despite the confident assertions of some writers. One Paris detective deduced from an unidentifiable fitting that victims were gassed in the little death-room. The more likely theory is that Doctor Petiot administered a fatal hypodermic injection, pretending that it was to protect the victim against typhoid or malaria in the country to which he believed he was being taken. The victim was then escorted to the death-room, into which his murderer could look through a hidden peep-hole while his victim died. The body was then dismembered, incinerated in the furnace or thrown into lime in the 'inspection pit'.

Except for the actual murder, what happened at the second interview could be deduced from what happened at

the first. A full report on this was submitted to the Paris
Gestapo by a young Jewish renegade. This episode, which
involves a kind of rough justice, proves the complicity of
some high-ranking Gestapo chief in what was going on. The
renegade was actually a Gestapo agent, saving his own life
at the cost of betraying other Jews. He was ordered by a
junior Gestapo official to investigate Doctor Petiot, and he
reported his first interview at Rue Lesueur; his report was
the basis of my account already recorded. Then he went
along for his second interview, and was never seen again.

His failure to file a second report left his immediate
Gestapo superior in a quandary. Perhaps Doctor Petiot *was*
engaged in the wholesale slaughter of French Jews—which
in German eyes was an innocent, indeed a laudable programme—or perhaps he really *was* smuggling Jews out of
France, and perhaps the agent had taken advantage of the
opportunity to escape from his reluctant service to the
Germans.

So the junior official reported his doubts to his superior
officer, and was surprised at the cold reception that greeted
him. It is now certain that his senior knew all about Doctor
Petiot, and was receiving a substantial rake-off for 'protection'. But with that interfering junior's report on the file,
the official had to pretend to take action on it. It was un-
avoidable that Doctor Petiot should be arrested; this was in
May 1943.

At the time of his arrest it would have been routine Gestapo procedure for the Rue Lesueur address, reported by the
Jewish agent, to be raided and thoroughly searched. If that
had happened a number of corpses in various stages of dismemberment would have been found. Doctor Petiot's
trial and execution for multiple murder would have followed,

so that the Germans could have kept up their pretence to French citizens that under the Occupation regime law and order were being strictly enforced.

But nothing happened! After a few months in custody the Doctor was released! The interfering and over-zealous junior official was transferred elsewhere; after which the corrupt senior official could sit back with an easier mind to enjoy the resumed flow of generous bribes and protection money from Rue Lesueur. Far from Doctor Petiot being a paid agent of some Gestapo official, that Gestapo official was a paid protector of Doctor Petiot!

III

After the Gestapo released him, towards the end of 1943, Doctor Petiot got back to work. But his previous long run of success, and his confidence in his corrupt German protector, made him careless. As a young medical student Petiot must have read newspaper reports of the Landru case. He must have known that quite early in his career of profitable murder Landru nearly crashed, when suspicious neighbours at Vernouillet complained of smoking chimneys when he was busy incinerating his women victims. He must have known, too, that some of the most telling evidence against this Bluebeard at his trial consisted of the records and mementoes of his victims which he had foolishly kept. It seems almost incredible that Petiot should have drawn public attention to himself in precisely the same way, and should similarly have kept the proofs that were eventually to help to send him to the guillotine.

On Saturday, March 11th, 1944, Doctor Petiot, after a busy week, thought he had better suspend operations—for the time being, at any rate. He looked round his basement boiler-room; noted with satisfaction the twenty-seven corpses in various stages of dismemberment that were evidence of twenty-seven highly profitable 'escape' deals. He stuffed as many limbs and torsos into the blazing furnace as it would hold; made sure that his breast-pocket held his latest collection of passports, ration books, and other documents that might fetch a price in the Black Market. Then he mounted his bicycle and rode home to the peace and quietness of his Rue Caumartin apartment—just a quiet, friendly, overworked Paris doctor, looking forward to a tasty dinner and a restful week-end.

That interfering junior Gestapo official had interrupted Doctor Petiot's career for a few months; an interfering neighbour ended it for ever. On that fateful Saturday thick black smoke belched forth from the chimneys of No. 21 Rue Lesueur smelling evilly of what the neighbour did not recognize as the characteristic odour of burning human fat. He complained to the *gendarmes*, and they in turn called the *pompiers*. Firemen broke into the house, but very soon came out again. "The place is full of dead bodies!" they told the police.

Doctor Petiot sighed resignedly as his quiet meal with his wife and son was interrupted by a summons from the police to return to Rue Lesueur. He jumped on his bicycle again and obeyed. In his awful basement he took the police sergeant aside. "This looks very incriminating," he explained reasonably. "Actually I am an executioner for the Resistance Movement. These are the corpses of German agents and collaborators."

The police-officer, a decent patriotic Frenchman himself, was inclined to be sympathetic. Pending such check as was possible on the pleasant doctor's story, he let him go. Doctor Petiot remounted his bicycle, rode off with no sign of perturbation until he was out of sight; then he began to pedal as hard as he could. That night he and his family left their apartment. By the time the police had referred to his criminal record and had rushed to Rue Caumartin he had left his wife and son with his brother in Auxerre and had disappeared. It was nearly eight months before he was traced.

Much had happened in the meantime. Five months after the police had raided the Rue Lesueur *abattoir*, Paris was liberated, and Doctor Petiot no longer had any hope of protection by the Gestapo. When some of his victims were identified as elderly wealthy Jews his story that he had been 'executing' German agents was seen to be ridiculous: these were definitely not types who would have helped the Jew-hating Nazis. And when news began to leak out that the Doctor had been engaged in deals with the Paris Gestapo, newspapers jumped, not unnaturally, to the wrong conclusions. "Petiot a Nazi Spy!" screamed the headlines. "Petiot a Gestapo Agent!" But they were wrong.

Those headlines were read with great indignation by a resident in the Rue Faubourg St Denis. He was an intrepid Resistance officer who called himself Capitaine Henri Valéry—a cautious and discreet officer, apparently, as he had not joined the Resistance movement until more than a month after the last German had been chased out of Paris. What so greatly irritated him was the fuss that was being made about the Petiot case—for political reasons, he claimed —and the unkind slurs on the name of a patriotic Paris doctor. Capitaine Valéry felt so strongly about the matter that he wrote a letter to a newspaper. The captain was in fact Doctor Petiot himself.

The letter attracted attention, because not many voices were being raised in praise of Doctor Petiot just at that time! Police collected the original letter from the newspaper office, and graphologists examined it. They decided that it was in the handwriting of the elusive Doctor Petiot, and Capitaine Valéry was arrested at a Métro station early in November 1944.

At his trial in Paris in March 1946 he was defended by the famous Maître René Floriot, but after a fortnight of hearing evidence and counsel the jury took only two and a half hours to find Doctor Petiot guilty of twenty-four of the twenty-seven murders with which he was charged.

Millions of Frenchmen still believe that Doctor Petiot was a German agent. I have shown that this was not true. He was a mass murderer, and but for his own carelessness he might have broken all records. The guillotine awaited him—twenty-four times by the official account, over sixty by his own. In the end the disparity did not matter.

On the morning of his execution, May 26th, 1946, he refused to take Holy Communion, and even declined the glass of rum offered to condemned men about to die in France. There was only one thing that troubled him as he hobbled at dawn towards the guillotine, with the neck of his shirt shorn away for the knife and his ankles shackled so that he could take only short, shuffling steps.

"Wait!" he pleaded. "I am in discomfort. I must make water."

"Do not trouble yourself, monsieur," said the executioner. "In an instant I shall have relieved all your discomfort."

TEN

The Queen's Doctor

I

THE REIGN OF QUEEN ELIZABETH I was an age of intrigue. In this the queen herself was no amateur, and the quality of her subtleties was enhanced by her woman's capacity to change her mind abruptly—often, immediately after she had made a decision. This confused her friends and enemies alike.

She was amply supplied with enemies. The Papal Bull deposing her had established her death as the objective of many fanatical Catholics, and plots, amateur though vicious, were frequently discovered throughout her reign. Sometimes mingled with, sometimes separate from, the Catholic conspiracies were the machinations of the King of Spain: nor were the supporters of Mary Queen of Scots ever idle.

In those days any monarch could expect assassination—Elizabeth more than the others, for recent history as well as her own personality had assured her of powerful and ruthless enemies. She was too mean to pay for an efficient Secret Service strong enough to protect her: she was very fortunate to have a faithful servant, Sir Francis Walsingham. He organized the first permanent spy and counter-spy system in Britain, though he often had to pay his agents out of his own pocket!

Walsingham had been an 'intelligencer' for the Cecils, that great family which served Elizabeth so well. Then, after a period as ambassador in France, he returned home to become a Privy Councillor. In those days this was no sinecure. The Council had only seventeen members, each of whom had charge of some department of the queen's administration.

Walsingham's official title was "a Principal Secretary". His task covered part of the work of a Foreign Secretary and the whole of that of the head of the Secret Service. The Cecils had employed spies: Walsingham organized them.

His greatest success concerned the Spanish Armada: it has been stated, indeed, that Walsingham knew of the project as soon as it entered King Philip's head. Certainly he was remarkably well informed about its progress—one of his men was actually working on the building of the great fleet at Malaga, sending home long ciphered reports inside wine-casks. The Armada was no surprise: the despair of the English leaders was the parsimony of the queen, who would allow no money to meet the threat.

This, however, was desperately serious: so were the constant plots against the queen's life. Walsingham countered many of these by a method now popular—he infiltrated his own agents among the conspirators. It was vitally important that Elizabeth should not die. Her legal successor was the Catholic Mary Stuart of Scotland, whose succession would have provoked civil war. Though she flirted with her courtiers, Queen Elizabeth had no thought of marriage, and could never have had the children who could have secured the

Protestant succession. Ben Jonson repeated a popular rumour of the day—supposedly emanating from the queen's doctor—when he declared that she had a maidenhead so tough that no man could mate her, though many had tried. She was a Virgin Queen despite herself.

Walsingham's successes were by no means uniform. He was a man affected by the weak and confused moral outlook of the day, and some of his victims deserve inclusion in a book such as this. The case of Doctor William Parry, M.P., will serve as an example.

Soon after the murder of William the Silent a Jesuit agent was apprehended on his way from Holland to Scotland. Hurriedly he ripped a piece of paper into fragments and flung them overboard. They were recovered and pieced together, and revealed the Papal scheme called "The Enterprise of England". This would have included the murder of Elizabeth and the establishment of a Catholic state.

Public feeling in England was deeply stirred by the revelation. Ardent patriots formed the "Bond of Association" threatening deadly retribution to *anyone* who would benefit by Elizabeth's death—which would include Mary Stuart and all her supporters, whether they had been involved in the murder or not. Parliament itself was swept by the emotional wave of loyalty, and proposed to legalize the Bond. But Elizabeth was against it: "no one must suffer for another's fault". Nevertheless, certain anti-Catholic measures were enacted: and the Member of Parliament for Queenborough, Doctor William Parry, attracted attention by his vehement protests.

Walsingham investigated the man, whom a rival had accused of high treason. This was the gravest offence under the law.

Legal outlook differed greatly from that of today: "better the guilty should escape than an innocent man should be condemned" is a comparatively novel maxim. In the sixteenth century the reverse applied—with especial force in Elizabeth's England. If the queen were murdered, not only would a Catholic succeed, but all the officers of state would have lost their jobs and probably their lives!

Parry was a man of poor reputation, with several prison terms to his discredit. He was arrested on the charge of plotting the queen's death. Evidence was meagre, so he was introduced to the rack. His nerve broke, and he confessed— only to deny his confession as soon as he had recovered his courage. It was, however, proved that the plot had Papal support, and this was enough to condemn Parry. Irate Members of Parliament held that the traditional fate of the traitor was too good for him, and wished to devise a special and more horrible end. But Parry's death, though ordinary by current legal standards, was bloody enough.

Later, Walsingham himself had doubts about Parry's guilt. The man had served as an English spy, and fresh evidence suggested that he was an *agent provocateur* rather than an assassin. He had sought to involve others in an imaginary conspiracy so as to denounce them—to his own profit. It was to some extent Parry's own fault that his fake plot was accepted as genuine. Quite apart from his confession in fear of the rack, he was such a liar that each of his statements contradicted the last. Even in Rome he had been accepted as a true and dedicated plotter—hence the Papal blessing. In effect, Parry was such a capable deceiver that no one could distinguish between his fact and his fiction, and in the emotional patriotism of the day only the damaging fiction was accepted.

II

Yet this episode was trifling compared with another.

Doctor Roderigo Lopez was a Jewish Portuguese whose family had been driven from Portugal by the Inquisition. He was a clever and well-qualified doctor, and settled down in London, one of his appointments being at St Bartholomew's Hospital. In his private practice he had to face much prejudice: he was a foreigner and he was Jewish. Nevertheless, such was his skill that some of the greatest in the land were numbered among his patients. They included the Earl of Leicester—and Sir Francis Walsingham.

Then, after seventeen years in England, he reached the pinnacle of distinction: he became physician-in-chief to Queen Elizabeth. He had long been a Christian; he was prosperous, lived in style in Holborn, and had a son at Winchester College.

There was another and better-known Portuguese refugee in England—Don Antonio, the pretender to the Portuguese crown, seized by the might of Spain. But his standing was low.

With the Armada defeated, the English leaders decided to make a counter-attack on Spain. Corunna would be raided, Portugal freed from the Spanish yoke, and Don Antonio placed on the throne. He was quite confident that the Portuguese would rise at his behest.

But they did not: the expedition was a dismal failure. And now, some years later, the discredited Don Antonio was living in poverty at Eton. He had sold all the family jewels, and now existed and fed his attendants sparsely on a miserable pension. Yet he was not entirely ignored: the anti-Spanish faction in England—led by the Earl of Essex— thought that he might still be of use at the right moment.

The Cecils, on the other hand, were doubtful; and were just as dubious about the value of any war, whether against Spain or any other country.

Another man had a decided opinion: King Philip of Spain. Holding that Don Antonio was potentially dangerous, he had fostered many plots against the pretender's life. All these were foiled; most of them were revealed by active English counter-spies.

Now, in 1593, interesting news reached Essex. A Portuguese named Ferreira, who had ruined himself in Don Antonio's cause, was living with Doctor Lopez in Holborn: and, said the report, he had turned traitor and had offered his services to Spain. He was arrested, but no evidence was produced, and no charge against him was made. By a peculiar decision he was placed in the charge of Don Antonio at Eton, a kind of house arrest. Further, British agents at the South Coast ports were instructed to keep a look-out for letters addressed to Ferreira and Doctor Lopez—those for Don Antonio were already seized and read.

Doctor Lopez went to the queen to plead for Ferreira, but failed. Now events moved rapidly. A neighbour of Lopez, named d'Avila, was arrested at Sandwich on his way home from Flanders. He carried a letter, in Portuguese, in ambiguous phrases. "The bearer will inform Your Worship in what price your pearls are held. I will advise Your Worship presently of the uttermost penny that can be given for them. Also the bearer shall tell you in what resolution we rested about a little musk and amber, the which I determined to buy. . . . If it shall please Your Worship to be my partner, I am persuaded we shall make good profit."

What did it mean? The phrases suggest some hidden code: the addressee proved to be non-existent. D'Avila could or would say nothing; but, taken under arrest to London, he asked a casual stranger to let Doctor Lopez know that he had been arrested.

Almost at the same time Ferreira, still held prisoner at Eton, managed to get a note to Doctor Lopez, warning him to prevent the journey of d'Avila from Flanders. Lopez replied, on a scrap of paper hidden in a handkerchief, that he had done his best to stop d'Avila. Both letters were read by Government spies.

Assuredly something crooked was afoot. Ferreira underwent a new interrogation. What was d'Avila's mission all about? The interrogators adopted an old trick—they persuaded Ferreira that Doctor Lopez had betrayed him. The foolish man began to talk.

Doctor Lopez, he said, had agreed to poison Don Antonio —whose son and heir would then agree a pact with Philip of Spain.

Then d'Avila was shown the rack. He broke down at once, and confirmed Ferreira's story. He himself was only a messenger, he said, between Ferreira and another Portuguese named Tinoco, who was a paid Spanish agent. The mysterious letter he carried related to the Don Antonio plot.

All this was very interesting, but there was little the English could do about it, save to guard Don Antonio. But some weeks later Lord Burghley, the queen's secretary, received a letter from this man Tinoco. The letter explained that he wished to see the queen, in order to reveal to her secrets of the highest importance, and asked for a safe conduct. Burghley gave him one—but as soon as Tinoco set foot in England he was arrested. As Burghley later explained, the safe conduct was "prudently drafted". It permitted Tinoco to come into England, but not to get out!

L

Tinoco had at one time been a follower of Don Antonio: but, despairing, he had been bribed to enter the Spanish Secret Service. He was interrogated by the Earl of Essex himself. He had come to warn the queen of an attempt on her life, he said; but later, under pressure, he admitted that he had been sent to England by his Spanish masters, to join Ferreira and to persuade Doctor Lopez to favour the Spanish cause.

Ferreira, d'Avila, Tinoco—all their stories pointed to Doctor Lopez! True, the conspiracy seemed to be directed against Don Antonio, but this could easily be a device to cover the murder of the queen. Who was better placed to carry out the deed than her physician?

Essex rushed to see Elizabeth. He was persuasive, and Doctor Lopez was arrested. He stood up firmly to questioning, however, and nothing incriminating was found in his house.

We have seen that the rivals of Essex were the Cecils. When he adopted a cause they opposed it almost automatically. So it was with Doctor Lopez. Essex had allowed his anti-Spanish obsession to run away with him: he saw spies and traitors everywhere, and even invented them. Sir Robert Cecil went to the queen. She was already distressed at the arrest of the doctor who had served her so well, and Cecil had no difficulty in persuading her that Lopez was innocent.

Essex was furious, but the four prisoners—Lopez, Ferreira, d'Avila, and Tinoco—were in his hands. He now abandoned simple interrogation and threatened his prisoners with the rack.

This was customary—especially in cases of treason, when all kinds of nefarious devices, from false evidence to torture, were employed to get a confession. It is strange that even highly intelligent men like Francis Bacon and Walsingham supported the legal use of torture.

Yet how could judges accept words forced from a man by excruciating physical pain? The fallibility of the method was exposed by a Polish nobleman. He killed his own horse, and then accused one of his servants of the crime. The man, under torture, admitted that he had killed the horse—until his master revealed the truth.

Essex, stung by the queen's doubts, was determined to drag the truth out of the conspirators. Lopez had defied the interrogators, but Ferreira and Tinoco were of weaker stuff. In fear of the rack, they incriminated each other—and Doctor Lopez.

The doctor had sold out to Spain, they declared—and he had agreed to poison the queen. This was Essex's triumph. Once more he hastened to Elizabeth.

He could add another character to the story of the conspiracy, he said. A Portuguese spy named Andrada, allegedly in the service of Don Antonio, had been sent by Doctor Lopez, and had seen King Philip. The latter had given him a diamond-and-ruby ring for Doctor Lopez, and had bade him support the conspiracy against the queen. And now Elizabeth's confidence in her doctor was for the moment shaken, for she recalled that he had earlier offered her a diamond-and-ruby ring, which she had declined.

Now Essex had a further basis for his interrogations. Doctor Lopez admitted the receipt of the ring, but said that the circumstances of the episode were quite different.

Andrada had been one of Walsingham's spies, he said: to give a respectable background to a mission to Spain, Lopez allowed his name to be used—Walsingham was a friend of his. Andrada was to explain to Philip that he had been sent by Doctor Lopez, who was well placed to kill the queen. The ring was indeed sent to Doctor Lopez, as a bribe for his aid.

This was quite a different story, typical of the intrigues of the day. Lopez had acted patriotically in allowing Walsingham to use his name, and so get the Spanish king incriminated in a plot against Elizabeth. One man, Walsingham, could destroy in a few seconds the case which Essex had built up.

But, alas for Lopez, Walsingham had died before the case had broken.

III

It was easy to ridicule Lopez's story. Obviously he had invented it to fit the evidence dragged out of his associates. And his plea of innocence depended upon the testimony of a dead man!

Even the Cecils now agreed that there was a serious case against him; and the doctor's heart was broken when he heard that Elizabeth had joined his accusers. The sight of the rack completed his discomfiture.

He became almost incoherent. One moment he denied his guilt, the next admitted it. He described fantastic and impossible plots, and in his ravings implicated dozens of other people. But nothing availed him.

Essex, however, was happy. He was the hero of the hour: he had exposed a dangerous plot against the beloved Elizabeth. And this aroused the old hatred of Spain once again: its king was a would-be murderer.

Doctor Lopez was adopted as a national whipping-boy—

a foreign traitor. Ballad-singers exposed his villainy in their doggerel verses. Any mention of his name was greeted by hisses. Had he not been safe in prison he would have been torn to pieces by the mob.

Some historians see him as the original of Shylock, but this is doubtful. Lopez was a European, a Christian, not a Hebrew financier. He was a cultured man, living quietly and in prosperity, not a miser who demanded his pound of flesh.

Doctor Lopez, Ferreira, and Tinoco were tried and condemned—the last vainly and pathetically claiming the protection of his "prudently drafted" safe conduct! But Elizabeth changed her mind once again, and refused to believe in her doctor's guilt. She defied the influence of Essex and the fury of the populace, and ordered the Lieutenant of the Tower not to surrender him for execution.

For two months her ban held firmly. The next episode is still shrouded in mystery. By one account Elizabeth weakened, frightened by the universal anger of the people; by another, Essex contrived to smuggle Lopez out of the Tower.

Whichever is the true version, on a fine June day in 1594 the three condemned men were tied to hurdles and dragged along Holborn—past the house of Doctor Lopez—to Tyburn. A huge crowd had assembled to enjoy the spectacle. Lopez attempted to make a speech from the scaffold—the conventional right of a condemned man. But the mob howled him down.

The executioner put the noose round his neck and pushed him off the scaffold. Gasping in terror, his face distorted, he swung in the air. Then, while still alive, he was cut down —for the legal revenge of the day demanded more than the death of a traitor.

The executioner ripped off the doctor's clothing and, to the delight of the crowd and the shrieks of the victim, castrated him. Next followed the process of disembowelling. He would not feel the third—his body was cut and slashed into four quarters, but he had already been beheaded.

Ferreira followed him to a death of similar barbarism. The unhappy Tinoco had beheld the fate of his colleagues— had been splattered with their blood and almost deafened by their cries. Now he must share their torture.

But he was cut down too soon. Young and strong, he regained his feet and attacked the executioner. The crowd howled with delight at this unexpected turn of events: the fickleness of a mob is proverbial. They cheered this man fighting so gallantly for his life, pushed aside the guards, and formed a ring. The executioner was easily getting the worst of the fight, but someone struck Tinoco down. Then guards held him down on the scaffold for the last act of the macabre scene—castration, disembowelling, and quartering.

IV

Doctor Lopez died as a traitor and a Spanish agent. But was he?

The answer is a reasoned negative. Almost certainly he was engaged in some nefarious project, but the letter captured on d'Avila suggests illicit commercial activities—smuggling, maybe, rather than espionage or treason. At the most the earlier episodes of the case could be interpreted as an attempt to persuade him to poison Don Antonio in return for a Spanish bribe. This would have been murder, but not treason. Hence it played but a minor part in the accusation and the trial. The latter depended almost entirely on the plot to kill

Elizabeth, as outlined by Andrada. Lopez's own explanation was dismissed with scorn. The only man who could have proved his story was dead. *But the story was true!*

Long, long after Lopez had been mauled to death, historians working in the Spanish archives chanced across some relevant papers.

Andrada, one of Walsingham's agents, had indeed visited Madrid. He saw, not Philip, but his Secretary of State. Andrada proffered the suggestion of a peace overture, but the Secretary had different ideas—and plenty of gold. He 'turned the spy round', to use the modern phrase. Andrada became a double spy. He was to report on conditions in England, and to try to persuade Doctor Lopez—using the diamond-and-ruby ring as a bribe—to rid the Spaniards of the inconvenient Don Antonio.

There was no mention at any time in the negotiations of the murder of Elizabeth. Not from any source, save the unreliable rack, is there any suggestion that Lopez would ever have betrayed his royal mistress. Why should he? For a Spanish bribe, would he give up his position, his salary, and the favour of the queen? And the risk of his detection would have been great. Had the queen been poisoned, the first suspicion would have been directed against the foreign Jew who was her physician.

So history exonerates Doctor Lopez from the charge for which he died so cruelly.

Long before then Elizabeth's own doubts had returned. The queen had a remarkable and penetrating intuition, especially when estimating the characters of men. She had had great confidence in Lopez, broken only occasionally by the urgent pleas of her advisers. Now, immediately after the execution, she regained her original confidence. Because of the nature of his crime Doctor Lopez had forfeited all his worldly goods, but Elizabeth allowed his widow to keep them. All save one item—the diamond-and-ruby ring with which Philip of Spain had sought to finance the conspiracy to murder her. She put it on her finger, and wore it until the day of her death.

ELEVEN

Woman Spy?

I

SOON AFTER THE SECOND WORLD WAR I was wandering about the ancient French province of Auvergne. It is a lovely land, but has had a stormy history. It was involved in endless wars—not only those of French kings, but those of the local barons; and, when these happened to be temporarily quiescent, in the more deadly wars of religion.

It is wild country, of mountains, forests, and valleys—ideal for guerrilla warfare. So when the Germans occupied Vichy France in 1942 the Auvergne Massif became a centre of the French Resistance forces.

When I got to Mende I found myself drawn into great argument. In the region round about the Maquis had been very active, its speciality being the shooting up of German convoys. After such an operation its members would disappear, and the Germans could never find them.

Thoroughly exasperated, the Nazis descended to a time-dishonoured device—they seized hostages, and tried using the usual ferocious methods to persuade them to talk. And the argument concerned one of these hostages.

Detachments of the Maquis usually took a *nom de guerre*, and one operating near Mende adopted that of Bir Hakim, after the scene of one of the first Free French victories in Africa. One night, as this company gathered for a raid on a convoy, it was surrounded by an overwhelming German force. Most of the French were killed. The rest were captured, marched into Mende, and all shot in front of the cathedral.

Who had betrayed the Bir Hakim company? Among the hostages taken by the Germans had been a priest. It was now believed that he had weakened under torture and had talked.

"You are interested in our differences?" asked an elderly man in a café.

"Very."

"It is a pity, but it has always been a habit of the French to quarrel among themselves. In Auvergne we were better than anybody else at this form of suicide."

"Now, Louis!" his wife warned. "You don't know what you're talking about."

"What? I do. What do you know about these things?"

Ten minutes later, the husband-wife contest temporarily stilled, our conversation returned to the subject of the underground war.

"All this talk about women Maquis soldiers is all bunk," said the old man. "But, I will admit, they were very useful with the commissariat. They used to bring baskets of food into the *causses*—our flat-topped mountains, you know."

"And there was Simone," said the wife.

"Yes, indeed. There was Simone. She has been discussed as fiercely as the priest today. Was she a collaborator, or a spy? Me, you understand, I would never believe that she betrayed us. Didn't she lead us to our greatest victory? But before that—there were people who did not trust her."

"And her own story?"

"She has never told it—at least, so I have heard. But she was a remarkable woman."

He added enough details to arouse my curiosity. She lived in a village a dozen miles out of Mende, he explained. I visited it—at first, casually: a pathetic place, a victim of the depopulation which has smitten this region of France. A third of the houses were deserted and in ruins.

It was not difficult to meet Simone. (I have deliberately omitted her surname.) Whatever the people of Mende thought about her, there was no question about the opinion of the villagers. The French recognize intellect, and hers was far above theirs. At the same time she was very practical. When I first arrived she was just giving expert aid to a cow making a difficult delivery of a calf. I was born on a farm, and could help. Our first fragments of conversation were very practical obstetric comments!

I went to her cottage for coffee, but it was clear that she was not disposed to talk. She interested me greatly: she would be about forty, with a drawn face as one who had known great pain. I made one or two hesitant approaches, but she changed the subject abruptly.

But my years in counter-espionage were not wasted. I am experienced in interrogation, and began among the villagers. From one and another I picked up fragments of information. Then I used an old trick—putting together all that I knew, I made it seem as if I knew a good deal more when I returned to Simone.

The device did not fail me. What follows is in the main Simone's story, with items of confirmation gathered locally, and a few of my own comments added. Even when Simone began to talk, our conversation had frequent halts while I soothed her misgivings. This, it will be remembered, was in 1946, when I had no thought of writing this book. But Simone's story deserves a place in it.

II

When war broke out Simone was a teacher in Montpellier. Well into her thirties, she had almost given up hopes of marriage; but she was devoted to the small children who were her pupils.

For the first winter the war seemed far away. Then came the overwhelming German attack and the collapse of France. To Simone this was indeed a bitter blow: never had she guessed that her country was so weak.

Montpellier was, of course, in that portion of the country we know as Vichy France. There were no Germans about, but life grew more and more difficult. In the towns especially: for long the townsfolk had exploited the peasant farmers, who now had their opportunity for revenge. The rationing system frequently broke down. True, there was always food available—at a price. But French teachers were not well paid.

It was to replenish her larder that she began to visit her home village in the *causse* country. She knew the farmers there, and usually managed to collect a supply of vegetables on her visits—meat was much more difficult. Then came the Allied landings in North Africa, and the German occupation of Vichy France. Now every difficulty was multiplied tenfold.

Soon after this time Édouard returned to the village. He had been wounded in the battles of 1940, and walked with a pronounced limp; he had taken advantage of the confusion in occupied France to make his way home.

He was younger than Simone; she had always liked him, and now sought him out on his father's farm. He was a man of great intelligence, and was glad to talk to her—the normal village conversation was very limited in scope.

Some months later Simone lay uneasily on her bed in her little flat in Montpellier, her mind tormented by the trials of her country. Suddenly she heard a gentle tapping on the window.

She jumped out of bed. "Who is there?"

"It's me—Édouard."

She let him in. He looked desperately tired. As she made coffee his story emerged. A friend had summoned him to Dijon. Would he undertake the formation of a Maquis group in the Margeride—the mountainous district north of Mende? There were few Germans there—only periodic patrols—so there would be little action, but the district was admirably fitted for the reception of supplies flown out by British aircraft.

Édouard had agreed. But on the return journey he had been picked up by a Gestapo patrol. In the night he had escaped, and had been on the run for forty-eight hours.

"I hoped to get home tonight," he said. "But I am exhausted—I should never arrive. Could you shelter me?"

"Of course."

"I shall have to stay until tomorrow night."

"Of course."

"I will sleep in this chair."

"You will sleep in my bed."

She did not avoid the next scene, but did not linger in her description of it. He had slept the night through, and had stayed in her flat during the day.

"You cannot go out," she declared, as she returned from

school. "The Germans are everywhere. There is something afoot—they may not be after you, but could get you by mistake."

He stayed. There was an argument as to which should use the single bed. Eventually both did.

She was a virgin, and no man had previously approached her. She gave herself to him gladly.

"But, alas," he said, as he prepared to go the following evening—she had reported the streets quiet—"when you come to the village you must not see me. If anything went wrong anybody who knew me would be in danger."

"What is danger?" she smiled, and gently pulled him again towards the bed.

Now she had to restrain herself, lest her friends should remark the glow of happiness in her eyes. And she did manage to see him in the village, by stealth; and twice he came to Montpellier. She was as happy as a woman could be in the midst of a war.

Anxious, nevertheless. Édouard was forming his Resistance group. The first drop of supplies had already been made, successfully. Many more would doubtless follow; and each one spelled danger.

III

When Lieutenant Heinz Hoffmann was seconded to service with the Gestapo he was angry. True, his days as an infantryman were over. He was a sentimental young man, and bitterly resented the fact that he had not been 'honourably wounded'—he had been knocked down by an ammunition wagon which had then passed over him, breaking both his legs.

He was no more than twenty, and looked less. Youth is resilient, and after his first disgust he grew interested in his job. At least he was not rounding up Jews for the concentration camps. These Resistance groups were just as much enemies as those the Germans fought in ordinary battle conditions.

He was an intelligent young man, and he spoke French well. And he was still a soldier, and obeyed orders. He had been told to establish contact with the Margeride Resistance group.

A local reconnaissance proved to be useless—none of these country yokels knew anything. But then a casual remark by one of his police prompted another approach. There was a woman teacher in Montpellier who came from the Margeride region. She was known to visit it in search of food—she must have friends there. And she was a good Pétainist: her tongue sharply criticized those who brought further misery to France by this ridiculous resistance to authority. He was not to know that this was a pose which Simone had adopted at Édouard's suggestion, to distract any possible suspicions.

Hoffmann made inquiries before he approached her. She had elderly parents at Lyon, and was anxious for them. And she was very practical. This decided his approach. Calling on Simone, he explained his needs. These Resistance groups were a menace to all Frenchmen, and only brought misery to their own countryside. He needed a contact with the Margeride. It could well be very discreetly arranged. And if she would undertake the task she would not only be working in the true interests of France; she would be paid, and her parents would receive the special rations which the Germans reserved for their friends.

She sought to gain time, so that she might consult Édouard

—had Hoffmann moved forward but one step in his argument she would have accepted his offer on the spot. For, when she learned that Edouard was delighted with the idea, Hoffmann went into more detail.

"At least I have a clue to the leader of the group," he said—and named Édouard!

It was probably from these days that Simone's reputation as a collaborator and a spy began. She made many journeys to Mende—but the information she brought back was supplied by Édouard. It suggested that the Resistance group was a feeble and irregular affair, and had had but meagre success. Later she did bring back news of supply drops, but always *after* they had happened.

"You have started well, Simone," Hoffmann declared. "We cannot expect immediate successes. One day we will hit these bumpkins hard."

This, duly reported to Édouard, prompted an idea. Actually his group was now strong, well organized, and well supplied with light arms. Yet he was concerned. Half a dozen volunteers had joined the group from Clermont-Ferrand. They were all Army men, and he suspected that they were deserters—and traitors. Action by a friendly local postmaster confirmed this—Édouard read a letter by one of the men.

He had already decided that the traitors should be tried and shot when he considered Simone's item of news. A scheme emerged which would bring justice to the traitors and would consolidate Simone in the confidence of Hoffmann.

He told only his trusted aides of his intentions. Then, when his group assembled by night south of Mende, he told them of a change of plan. The drop for the night had been postponed, he said; instead, he planned an attack on the gaol at Mende, where some doughty freedom fighters were imprisoned. The group was divided into sections. The traitors formed one, under a local leader. They carried, not rifles like the rest, but explosives to blow in the strong doors of the prison.

The change of plan was not really as sudden as Édouard pretended, and a warning had been passed by Simone to the Germans. The sections separated to their different tasks, but only the traitors carried on; the remainder of the sections went quietly home. The seven men—the leader had to be sacrificed in order to give the necessary authority to the plan —approached the prison, to be met by withering machine-gun fire. One bullet struck a packet of explosive, with disastrous results.

The Germans were delighted: this was their first victory in this part of France. Lieutenant Hoffmann was congratulated by his superior officer, and rushed round to thank Simone.

"He was only a boy. By the way he talked you would have thought that he had won the War. He was so excited that he embraced me. I think it was by accident, but one of his hands found my breast.

"I could sense his discomfort: he was only a lad, and had never had a woman. His hand returned to my breast—and this time it was purposeful.

"He was burning for me. And why not? I wanted to gain his utter confidence. My body meant nothing—considering what I was doing, I might be dead any day. And actually I was already carrying Édouard's child. Heinz did not know this. Nor did he notice anything when I allowed him to undress me. Poor lad! He had never seen a woman before, and in his eagerness he ripped off my clothes. He came to my breast like a baby.

M

"Heinz wanted to come again next day, but I would not let him.

"The dead men by the prison were not identified. Not until much later did the Germans learn that they had executed their own agents!"

Now, it could be well understood, Simone was excellently placed. But I was surprised at the next incident.

"I know that I was given credit, but I had nothing to do with it," she said. "The Resistance groups had plenty of friends in Montpellier, and when the Germans began to prepare a convoy for a grand sweep through the region it could not be hidden. The groups were warned; but when would it start and where would it go? I do not know who found out, and how, but not all the Germans kept their mouths shut. Anyway, when it moved across the Margeride by night Édouard and his men were ready and in force.

"There are one or two men here in the village who could give you details. As I understood it, Édouard laid mines in a mountain road north of here. These blew up the troop carriers which headed the convoy, and brought the whole lot to a halt. Then Édouard's men, from higher up the mountain, opened fire with a trench mortar and sub-machine guns. The Germans, over-confident, had asked for trouble and got it. They were in utter confusion, and nearly a hundred were killed. It was one of the Maquis' biggest victories."

"But you had nothing to do with it?"

"No. I had deliberately laid off my visits to Édouard for a time."

But she was concerned with the next incident—by accident. Heinz was hopelessly in love: the fact that Simone was nearly twice his age apparently meant nothing.

He showed his affection in one peculiarly practical way. He was nervous for her safety. If the Resistance leaders got to know that she was actually working for the Germans, her end would be unpleasant: discipline in unconventional war must be strict. When she reported on Resistance activities, therefore, he 'edited' the reports before passing them on—deliberately making them inaccurate. Hoffmann did not know, of course, that they were already inaccurate when they reached him.

I suppose it was bound to happen—though Simone knew nothing of her lover's actions on her behalf. After one of her visits to the Margeride she reported to Hoffmann that a drop was expected on Wednesday. He, assuming that her information was correct, altered the day to Tuesday—which *was* correct. Thus the Germans were there at the right time, captured the entire drop of arms, and killed three of the Resistance group.

"And it was my fault," she said sadly.

"I don't see that. You did not know that your reports were amended."

"No. But some of my friends thought that I had betrayed them."

"At least the Germans would be pleased with you."

"I suppose so."

"Hoffmann must have been delighted."

"No."

"What?"

"He was in prison."

Officers can never hope to hide their love affairs from their men. The fact that Lieutenant Hoffmann had fallen for a French teacher twice his age had become a stock joke among the local Germans. Hence, when a senior officer arrived from Dijon to investigate the disaster of the convoy, he soon picked up this interesting item of news.

Hoffmann was arrested. He was a poor liar, and made no attempt to disguise his interest in her. She too was interrogated. She denied that she had anything to do with the convoy, but could not deny that she had acted as an intermediary between Hoffmann and the Resistance.

The inference seemed to be all too obvious. Hoffmann was shot as a traitor.

Simone was visibly distressed as she described this episode. She had obviously been fond of Hoffmann—perhaps a maternal love mingled with physical passion.

"And Édouard?"

"He was killed—in the first operation mounted by Heinz's successor."

"I am sorry. And—your child?"

"Born dead."

Poor woman! No wonder her face was drawn: her little world had disintegrated.

I murmured my sympathy. "And even some of your friends call you a spy."

"I was never a spy, monsieur. I was just a woman."

TWELVE

The Strange Case of Alger Hiss

I

THE CASE OF ALGER HISS, the most baffling in the long and murky history of espionage, presents several unusual features.

Most unusual, perhaps, was the status of the protagonists. The accuser was a highly paid American journalist, a senior editor of the magazine *Time*. The accused was a brilliant lawyer who, as a State Department official, had accompanied President Roosevelt to the Yalta conference with Marshal Stalin, and had organized the San Francisco conference of the United Nations.

This was not the familiar type of spy trial in which an obscure civil servant, like the Englishman Harry Houghton or Bunty Gee or William John Vassall, is charged on the information of anonymous counter-espionage agents. The Hiss case was a battle of giants. No wonder it became headline news from the start.

Unusual, too, was the fact that although scores of millions of Americans accepted the implication that Hiss had been guilty of espionage, he was never tried for that offence, which had become time-barred under United States law.

And the defence allegation of "forgery by typewriter", of which even more sensational suggestions were advanced after than before the trial ended, is unique in criminological history.

The rather confusing sequence of legal proceedings in the Hiss case was as follows:

1.   Whittaker Chambers, a witness summoned before the House of Representatives Committee on Un-American Activities, testified that he knew Alger Hiss to have been a Communist (August 1948).

2.   Challenged by Hiss to repeat his allegations in public, the witness did so, and Hiss instituted proceedings for slander (September 1948).

3.   In his defence the witness produced documents which appeared to prove not merely that Hiss had been a Communist, but that he had been a Soviet spy (November 1948).

4.   On the evidence of the documents, the Department of Justice intervened and placed the case before a New York grand jury investigating espionage allegations, who took evidence from Hiss and from his accuser (December 1948).

5.   The grand jury believed the accuser and disbelieved Hiss; this implied belief that he had been guilty of espionage. But that offence was time-barred under the Statute of Limitations. Hiss was then indicted for having given perjured evidence before the grand jury (December 1948).

6.   At a first trial for perjury the jury disagreed (May–July 1949).

7.   At a second trial for perjury Hiss was convicted, sentenced to five years' imprisonment, but released on bail pending an appeal (November 1949 to January 1950).

8.   The appeal failed (December 1950).

9.   Hiss went to prison (March 1951).

10.   An application for a fresh trial on the grounds of newly discovered evidence was rejected (January 1952).

Thus the man who may—or may not—have been one of the most highly placed Soviet agents to have operated in the Western world was punished for an offence different from that of which the majority of his fellow-citizens believed him guilty.

II

Much of the widespread public interest in the case lay in the characters of the two men mainly involved, especially in that of the accuser, David Whittaker Chambers. When the story broke he was a short, plump, sallow forty-seven-year-old ("This little round man", as he described himself), with the easy and apparently imperturbable manner one might expect of such an experienced journalist as the $30,000-a-year senior editor of *Time*.

But beneath the smooth surface of Chambers's self-control, as he staggered the nation with his sensational revelations, his sensitive mind must have been scarred by memories of his appalling childhood. It is significant that he tried to commit suicide before the case ended.

The grandfather of David Whittaker Chambers was a drunkard, and his grandmother was insane. His father was

an artist, who deserted his family after fights with the grandmother, an old lady who was apt to settle domestic differences
by grabbing a knife or a pair of scissors. David's mother had
been a temperamental actress, who was so nervous that she
always went to bed with an axe, and little David used to sleep
with a knife under his pillow. If his mother heard a noise in
the night she would start to scream, and tell the children,
David and his brother, to scream too. At a fairly early age
David's brother took to drink, tried to involve David in a
suicide pact, and eventually, after some unsuccessful at-
tempts, managed to gas himself.

After leaving Columbia University, David Whittaker
Chambers was dismissed from his first job for stealing books.
In 1924, when he was twenty-three, he joined the Communist
Party and was given a job on the American *Daily Worker*
newspaper, of which he became editor three years later. And
four years after that he was taken into the secret section
of the Party, which meant in effect that he became a Soviet
agent.

He then had to sever all open connection with the Party
and its members, to use a confusing series of false names, and
to learn such espionage techniques as photographing borrowed secret documents. For protection he carried a concealed sheathknife. He began to act as go-between with
traitors in Government departments, through whom he
obtained copies of secret documents for transmission to his
Russian superiors and eventually to Moscow.

There is no reasonable doubt as to the truth of what
Chambers said about himself up to the year 1934. From then
onward Alger Hiss enters the picture, and the conflicting
stories told by him and Chambers become almost impossible
to disentangle—a battle of acute wits involving what was

called by the Earl Jowitt, Britain's ex-Lord Chancellor, "massive and monumental lying" by either or both of the protagonists.

What Whittaker Chambers said was that in mid-1934 a Washington Communist leader introduced him to a fellow-Communist and potential underground worker ("a disciplined and dedicated Communist" according to Chambers) —Alger Hiss.

III

In 1934 Alger Hiss was thirty years old, a brilliant young lawyer even at that early stage of his career. There seems to have been a streak of instability in the Hiss family—as there undoubtedly was in the Chambers family—as both the father and sister of Alger Hiss committed suicide. But after a splendid educational record Alger had grown into a tall, dark, good-looking young man with a serious and intelligent expression.

If the evidence of Chambers be accepted he must have known Hiss fairly intimately, and he described him as "a man of great simplicity and great gentleness and sweetness of character", and as "a charming personality, absolutely sincere in his convictions, and motivated by the idea that he was on the right track".

Except for Mrs Hiss, the families play little part in the story; but, for the record, Chambers had a wife, Esther, an ex-Communist trade-union secretary, and two small sons. Hiss had married Priscilla, a widow of Quaker stock and rather Left-wing views, and he had a son and a stepson.

At the time of his first meeting with Chambers, Hiss was Legal Assistant to the Nye Committee, which was investigating the American armaments trade. A year later he was

transferred to the office of the Solicitor-General. And a few
months after that he became assistant to the head of an
important section of the State Department—the American
equivalent of the British Foreign Office. According to Chambers, Hiss was passing him information and documents from
the time he served with the Nye Committee, but the legal
proceedings were mainly concerned with State Department
documents allegedly passed to Chambers for transmission
to the Russian spy network during 1937 and part of 1938.

During 1938 Chambers became disillusioned with Communism. He decided to break with his Soviet paymasters and
underground Party contacts and, he said, tried to persuade
Hiss to do likewise. Hiss refused and, Chambers suggested,
may have remained a Communist for the next ten years. In
the meantime Hiss was rising higher in Government service.
In mid-1939 he became assistant to the Government Adviser
on Political Relations, and in 1944 he entered the Office of
Special Political Affairs. After organizing the Dumbarton
Oaks Conference, at which the United Nations Charter was
drafted, he became Director of OSPA and was chosen to
accompany President Roosevelt to the conference at Yalta
with Marshal Stalin and Winston Churchill.

For different purposes both pro-Hiss and anti-Hiss
writers have exaggerated the importance of the part played
by Hiss at Yalta. The general picture conveyed is that
shrewd, ruthless Marshal Stalin was faced by an American
President who was then practically a dying man, with Hiss,
as Presidential Adviser, whispering into Roosevelt's ear—
either urging him to stand firm for American interests
(say the pro-Hissers) or persuading him to agree to cunning
Russian proposals to double-cross the United States (say the
anti-Hissers).

Hiss did not, in fact, direct United States policy at Yalta. But, if he had been a Soviet agent, he could, of course, have given the Russians useful advance information as to forthcoming American moves in the battle of wits. So it is not surprising that many angry Americans later believed—rightly or wrongly—that it was the presence of a sinister Soviet agent in the Presidential entourage that led to the Western nations being outsmarted by the Russians at Yalta.

Here we should consider whether, in fact, the Western nations *were* outmanœuvred at Yalta. The agreement very often bore the Stalin stamp, and changed the face of Europe: the new shape of Germany and Poland could prove to be the cause of the next war; or, failing this, its occasion. Some of the details of the agreement may also prove to be far more important than was realized at the time. The Kurile Islands, for example, were handed over to the Soviet Union. These islands had been a major Japanese base during the Second World War; the largest of them, Etorofu, was the assembly point for the attack on Pearl Harbor.

It is known that today the Russians have restored and improved the fortifications, rebuilt sixteen airfields, and enlarged the submarine base.

Maybe the shrewd Stalin had been so impressed by the shattering attack on Pearl Harbor that he visualized a future onslaught—made by Russia. In a future war the threat from the Kuriles might keep the American forces too busy to allow the United States to launch its full strength in European operations. *If* Alger Hiss were a spy he would have had no great difficulty in persuading Roosevelt to let Russia have the Kuriles. Roosevelt was thinking of a peaceful future, not another war.

In those days important developments in international

relations were taking place in swift succession. And always near their centre was Alger Hiss. When the United Nations Charter was signed at the San Francisco Conference in June 1945 he was Secretary-General and, in co-operation with the FBI, was in charge of the security arrangements. In December of the following year he was adviser to the United States delegation in London at the first meeting of the United Nations Assembly.

Early in 1947 Hiss resigned from Government service and was elected President of the wealthy Carnegie Endowment for International Peace, at a salary of $20,000 a year. He held that position until Chambers blasted his brilliant career in August 1948.

IV

To return to Whittaker Chambers: during 1938 he made his preparations to break with underground Communism and espionage with great care and much forethought. "I had sound reason for supposing that the Communists might try to kill me," he said. And, whatever opinion we may form of the reliability of his later testimony on oath—he having by then graduated from atheism through Episcopalianism to Quakerism—it is obvious from his own admissions that in late 1938 he was still as unscrupulous a double-crosser in his own interests as he had previously been in those of his Russian spy-masters.

Firstly, he said, he needed a car as a means of flight from Soviet punishment squads. For this purpose he borrowed $400 from Hiss, who thought that Chambers needed a car for his espionage work. Hiss denied this, and said that $400 which Priscilla Hiss drew from the bank a few days before the car was bought was not lent to Chambers, but was used to buy furniture for a new house. In this, as in practically every other episode of the Hiss trial, we come up against a tangle of contradictory evidence that can only be described as baffling. That withdrawal of $400 reduced the Hiss bank account to a few dollars, which was reasonable if he were furnishing his new house, but unlikely if he were providing a hard-up Communist with a new car. But, if the story told by Hiss were true, it is strange that he should have withdrawn money for furniture before the house had even been advertised for sale. But, again, there was something rather phoney about the whole transaction, as Hiss had signed a lease of the house three days before the publication of the advertisement. Checking hundreds of such contradictory details in the various stages of the Hiss trials simply gets us nowhere.

Having acquired his escape car, with funds from an unknown source, Chambers next needed what he called "life-preservers". This apparently meant a *cache* of secret papers hidden in a place known only to himself; so that if he were ever threatened with reprisals by the spy-ring, he could issue a counter-threat to produce the papers and prove the activities of the ring and the identities of its members. So, during the last months of his association with Hiss, Chambers declared, he regularly collected from Hiss copies of borrowed State Department documents, which had been copied by Priscilla Hiss on her Woodstock typewriter. He had had them photographed by the spy-ring photographer, then handed the photographs to his Russian spy-master and kept the identifiable typed copies as "life-preservers". And, if the story were true, the effectiveness of those precautions in 1938 was demonstrated ten years later when they ruined Hiss, and when other members of the alleged spy-ring were

publicly named, including the publicity-shunning Colonel
Bykov of the Soviet Secret Service.

After lodging his "life-preservers" in a relative's home,
"For a year I lived in hiding," said Chambers, "sleeping by
day and watching through the night with gun or revolver
within easy reach. That was what underground Communism
could do to one man in the peaceful United States in the
year 1938."

Pro-Hiss critics of Chambers have quoted that statement
as an indication that the small boy from a psychologically
unhealthy home had grown into a pathological liar with a
persecution complex, who imagined murderous Communist
bogy-men under every bed, waiting to pounce. But, in fairness
to Chambers, it should be recalled that at about the period of
his defection, in the late nineteen-thirties, sinister things
were happening in America. The murder-squads of Stalin's
Department for Special Tasks—nicknamed the Travelling
Executioners—were beginning in the United States a cam-
paign of assassination of renegade Communists, bringing
across the Atlantic the terrorist methods which they had
been using for years in Europe. Examples of murders whose
full significance many Americans may not have appreciated
at the time were those of Juliet Poyntz, Carlo Tresca, and
Louis Adamic, and the 'suicide' of Walter Krivitsky.[1]
Chambers's fear of death was amply justified.

In 1938 and again in 1945 Chambers made statements to
security officers, and among alleged Communists in Government service he named Alger Hiss. But Hiss's denial that he
was a Communist was accepted by his superiors. Then on
August 3rd, 1948, Chambers was summoned to appear before
the House of Representatives Committee on Un-American

[1] See *Spy Mysteries Unveiled*, by Vernon Hinchley.

Activities—which it will be less of a mouthful to call the House Committee—and Alger Hiss was doomed.

V

It might seem that the scope of the House Committee's inquiries was rather difficult to define, as would be un-British or un-Ecuadorian or un-Pakistani activities. And however un-American might appear the activities of the murderous Mafia or the inheritors of the Al Capone tradition, the Committee concentrated on a hunt for Communists and fellow-travellers. A dozen or so of Communist officials confessed to the Committee what they had been publicly preaching for years; but a similar number of Hollywood script writers took advantage of their right under the Constitution to refuse to answer questions that might incriminate them.

Rupert Furneaux wrote in *Courtroom USA 2*, in connection with the Hiss case: "In its ten years of existence it [the Committee] had achieved little. It was 'floundering in failure and ridicule', in the words of an acute political observer." The observer was Alistair Cooke of BBC "Letter from America" fame, and what he actually wrote in his book on the case was that such an impression of the Committee's activities would have been wrong. But Rupert Furneaux's inaccurate quotation does, in fact, indicate what many Americans were thinking at the time.

So it was stimulating for the increasingly discouraged Committee when Whittaker Chambers appeared before them as a genuine and helpful Soviet ex-spy with sensational stories of treason in high places. This was good stuff, and would at least entitle them to apply for a renewal of their financial grant. And nobody stressed the fact that the allegations now

made in public had lain gathering dust in some Government
pigeonhole for the past ten years.

But the most sensational of Chambers's revelations were
yet to come. To the Committee he merely named Alger Hiss
as a Communist who had held high office under the Government. But that was enough for the reporters, one of whom
telephoned Hiss that night to invite his comments. His
reply was immediately to ask the Committee to hear what
he had to say for himself.

What he had to say was definite enough: "I am not and
never have been a member of the Communist Party. I do not
and never have adhered to the tenets of the Communist
Party. I am not and never have been a member of any
Communist front organization. I have never followed the
Communist Party line, directly or indirectly." And as to
Whittaker Chambers: "So far as I know I have never laid
eyes on him."

Confronted later with Chambers, Hiss at first continued
to maintain that he had never seen him before. There ensued
a protracted and unconvincing scene when Hiss listened carefully to the way Chambers spoke, inspected him physically,
made him open his mouth and asked what recent dental work
he had had done. It all gives an impression that Hiss found,
on seeing Chambers, that he needed time to work out his
story, hence his desperate pose of non-recognition. In the
end Hiss admitted that Chambers might be a man whom he
had known slightly in the nineteen-thirties as "George
Crosley", a "deadbeat" journalist who had contacted him
in connection with his official duties, which included issuing
hand-outs to the Press.

Assessment of the reliability of testimony is often best
achieved by watching the demeanour of a witness. But in the

case of highly intelligent men accustomed to concealing their emotions, their precise words under questioning are often as well worth studying. For instance, according to the record, Hiss prefaced his answers to questions with "As far as I remember", "To my best recollection", and similar qualifications no less than 198 times. A member of the Committee sneered, "You are a very agile young man, Mr Hiss." But, in the circumstances, he could hardly have expected this experienced lawyer and senior public servant to make hasty and ill-considered statements.

Some of the replies of Chambers were no less significant. For instance, when Hiss asked him if he had ever called himself George Crosley he answered, "Not to my knowledge." That was a peculiar form of words. A man who had admitted using a series of false names might truthfully have said, "Not that I remember." But "Not to my knowledge" implies that something had happened of which the witness was not aware at the time, which could not possibly apply to the use of an alias. And Chambers was not a woolly-minded semi-illiterate; he was an experienced senior journalist, accustomed to weighing the precise meaning of every word and phrase he used in the highly compressed columns of *Time*.

The verbatim report of the proceedings clearly indicates that some members of the Committee became hostile to Hiss; this was, perhaps, particularly understandable in the case of Senator Nixon, a Quaker like the newly converted Chambers. He said to Chambers later in a private conversation, "If the American people understood the real character of Alger Hiss they would boil him in oil," a somewhat un-Quakerlike remark.

In their interim report the Committee recorded their

N

opinions of the manner in which the two witnesses had given their evidence—Chambers as "forthright and emphatic", and Hiss as "vague and evasive". But if the witnesses' selection of the spoken word bore any relation to their selection of the written word, it could be suggested that what we detect in their manner of testifying are habits of self-expression engendered by their respective professions.

In his blunt way Congressman Hebert summed up the position as he saw it at that date: "Mr Hiss, either you or Mr Chambers is lying. And whichever one of you is lying is the greatest actor that America has ever produced." Those words remained true throughout the case of Alger Hiss.

The end of Act One came when Hiss strode towards his accuser and said, "I would like to invite Mr Whittaker Chambers to make these same statements out of the presence of this committee without their being privileged for libel." As a result Chambers was invited to repeat his allegations in a radio programme called "Meet the Press". And scores of millions of listeners heard him say, "Alger Hiss was a Communist, and may still be one."

So, by what would seem to have been an unnecessary and dangerous challenge if he were a guilty man, Hiss had placed himself in the position of being practically forced to sue Chambers for slander. This he did, claiming no less than $75,000 damages. And up to this stage Chambers had never suggested that Hiss was a spy, merely that he had been a Communist.

There is an American procedure under which, in such cases, one of the parties can cross-examine the other in "pre-trial proceedings". But before he could be questioned under this procedure Chambers went to the Brooklyn address of a relative where, ten years earlier, he had hidden an envelope. He claimed that this contained his "life-preserver" documents. The relative took the envelope from its hiding-place behind a dumb-waiter and handed it to Chambers, "an envelope that was big, plump and densely covered with the clotted cobwebs and dust of a decade," wrote Chambers. And a ten-year accumulation of dirt shaken off on to the floor made such a mess that the relative had to get dust-pan and brush to clean it up. In the meantime Chambers went into the kitchen, opened the envelope, and, he says, took out his "life-preservers". These became known for convenience as the "Baltimore documents", as they were first produced to the lawyers in that city. They, especially those that were typewritten, provided the main evidence against Alger Hiss. In his book on the case ex-Lord Chancellor Earl Jowitt wrote: "The real case against Alger Hiss rested, and in my opinion must rest, upon the typewritten documents."

It seems to me that, from the almost inextricable tangle of conflicting evidence, we could decide definitely whether Hiss was innocent or guilty if only we knew what happened during the minute or two when Chambers was left alone in that Brooklyn kitchen. As Hiss later claimed that the Baltimore documents had been "forged by typewriter", and as it appears impossible that Chambers could have had time or opportunity during 1938 to rebuild a 'doctored' typewriter or to spend hours secretly copying the documents on the machine belonging to Priscilla Hiss, then Chambers's only chance to make documents produced to the Court in 1948 appear to have been hidden since 1938 was to take them from his pocket when he was alone in the kitchen for the brief period during which his relative was busy sweeping up. There was independent evidence of the retrieving of the envelope from its hiding-place, and of the conveyance of its

N*

alleged contents to the lawyers. But now that Chambers is dead there is nobody in the world who can say whether the documents that were the main cause of the ruin and imprisonment of Alger Hiss were taken from Chambers's envelope or from Chambers's pocket. The case depends on that detail.

In his book *Witness* Whittaker Chambers described his emotions as he saw the thick batch of papers. He said he felt dizzy for a moment and afraid he might fall. He gripped the edge of the kitchen table "in the kind of physical hush that a man feels to whom has happened an act of God". But if his memory was good enough to recall every little detail of the furniture and decorations of the Hiss home after ten years, surely he would have remembered and been prepared for the sight of the "life-preservers" he had carefully selected and hidden in order that, if need arose, he could produce them and ruin the only two people they implicated—Alger and Priscilla Hiss. Chambers's account of the incident seems to me to be hypocritical nonsense.

If his purpose were "life-preservation", why did his documents concern Hiss only? Why were the other traitors working for Chambers not involved? And, above all, why did not Chambers deposit "life-preservers" against the Russian and American Communists who employed *him*? They were the ones most likely to attack him when he deserted their ranks. There would be common sense in a plan whereby if they moved against him they would be promptly denounced by his cache of documents, Hiss could never harm him— could only denounce Chambers by exposing himself.

Lawyers acting for Hiss asked Chambers if he could produce any documentary evidence that Hiss was or had been a Communist. Chambers laid on the table the Baltimore papers, which included many sheets of typescript which experts later said had been typed on the machine belonging to Priscilla Hiss, and some sheets of manuscript notes in handwriting that Hiss admitted to be his own. All were copies or *précis* of confidential State Department papers. "Only these!" said Whittaker Chambers.

The lawyers were appalled. This looked like cast-iron proof, not merely that Hiss had been a possibly passive Communist sympathizer, but that he had been an active Soviet agent. As soon as Hiss was informed of the production of the Baltimore documents he insisted that they be placed at the disposal of the United States Attorney-General. It would not seem to have been the instinctive reaction of a guilty man.

Shortly afterwards the investigators of the delighted House Committee went to a small farm owned by Chambers to see what other deadly documents might be in his possession. He led them to his kitchen garden, where among a patch of growing pumpkins was one that had been hollowed out to form a hiding-place. Inside the pumpkin were rolls of microfilm of other State Department papers. It was every reporter's dream. "The Pumpkin Papers!" screamed the headlines. And before the Court had decided whether or not Chambers was guilty of slander, public opinion had decided that Hiss was guilty of treason.

There were, of course, pro-Hiss as well as anti-Hiss newspapers, and there developed one of those regrettable features of the American way of life called 'trial by newspaper'. As a distinctly pro-American British cousin, I think it is high time that the great, fair-minded United States adopted the strictly enforced British ban on newspaper comment on cases that are *sub judice*. I need quote only an episode in the case of John George Haigh, the acid-bath murderer, in

1949, three months after the production of the pumpkin papers. After Haigh's arrest, when reporting was permissible but comment became forbidden until after the verdict, statements that might have prejudiced the outcome of the trial were published in the mass-circulation London newspaper *Daily Mirror*. Three weeks later the company owning the paper was fined £10,000, and the editor was sent to prison for three months. The action was tough, but it was a manifest effort to be fair to an accused man who had to be presumed innocent until he was found guilty. That was a question for the court, not for Fleet Street, to decide.

Millions of words have been written about the case of Alger Hiss, and it is impossible in this chapter to do more than glance at one or two of the more important of many details of the mass of conflicting evidence. Chambers admitted that he had been a Soviet agent, and said that he had had five informants in the State Department, one of whom was Hiss. But Hiss maintained that he had merely become casually acquainted with Chambers—as the deadbeat George Crosley—in the course of his duties, when he had extended him a few small favours. It accordingly seemed important to establish whether the two men had been more closely associated than Hiss would ever admit; whether the Baltimore documents had been copied for Chambers by Priscilla Hiss on her own typewriter; or whether they had been forged years later as a weapon with which Chambers, if he ever got into trouble, could first threaten and then 'frame' Hiss.

As to the degree of intimacy between the two men, Chambers clearly had a detailed knowledge of the lay-out and contents of the Hiss home in Washington, where he said he used to call to collect documents every week or ten days, and had once stayed, with his wife, for several weeks.

Hiss denied the regular visits, but said that Chambers and his wife had once occupied his former apartment at a time when it became vacant, the Hisses having moved to a house they had bought, and the rent of the apartment having been paid in advance for a period which had not expired. Hiss also said that he had paid gas, electricity, and telephone charges for the period when the Chambers were in occupation. He was, he said, just doing a good turn to an impecunious and unsuccessful journalist who was having no luck in selling his articles to newspapers.

But, if Hiss were telling the truth, why on earth should he let his home and furniture be used by a deadbeat with whom he was only briefly and casually acquainted, not only letting him use the accommodation, which admittedly cost him nothing, but paying charges for public services out of his own pocket?

Yet if, on the other hand, Chambers were telling the truth, he acted with a provable regularity (which implies a lack of caution) unprecedented in the actions of any known Soviet Secret Service agent. He could have been seen and identified by neighbours as having called at the Hiss home every week or ten days, not merely once but sometimes twice a night— once to collect copies of documents typed by Priscilla Hiss, and sometimes again later to return documents after they had been photographed by "Felix", the spy-ring photographer in Baltimore. Challenged in court, Chambers agreed that when he had to make two double journeys between Washington and Baltimore—collecting, conveying, processing, and returning documents—it took him about nine or ten hours: say, from 5 P.M. to 2 A.M.!

Normal Russian Intelligence procedure is to avoid ever connecting an individual with an address. It is almost incredible that so intelligent a man as Chambers, if he had had the slightest and sketchiest Intelligence grooming, would have risked implicating Hiss by calling so regularly at his apartment. He would have met him in some isolated spot, a public park perhaps, and transferred borrowed documents in circumstances designed to make things difficult for any watching counter-espionage agents. And original documents, not copies, would have been handed over and later returned. That would have saved time and trouble, as well as the risk of typing errors Priscilla Hiss might make in copying the documents. The Russian spy-master, Colonel Bykov, would have greatly preferred photographs of originals to photographs of possibly inaccurately typed copies.

Hiss's story of the sublet apartment is not very convincing. But Chambers's story is wildly improbable—a defiance of strict basic safety rules imposed by the Soviet Secret Service on its agents.

Chambers also stated that Hiss had given him an old car, suggesting that it might be useful to some Communist organizer in his work if he were too poor to afford one of his own. Hiss agreed that he had disposed of an old car when he bought a new one, but said that he had sold it to a firm of car dealers and had had the transfer officially recorded. Ownership of the car was eventually traced, not to Chambers and not even to the car dealers—whose books contained no record of the transaction—but to a man who denied ever having seen Hiss and refused to testify further on the grounds that he might incriminate himself. What really happened about the car remains a mystery.

That discarded Hiss car was, of course, a different one from that which Chambers said Hiss had later lent him money to buy.

So it may be agreed, even if we skip a great deal of similarly inconclusive evidence, that the degree of intimacy between Hiss and Chambers remains in considerable doubt.

The most important evidence in the whole case was that as to the source of the Baltimore documents. These included sixty-five sheets of typescript and four sheets of memoranda in the handwriting of Hiss. The latter turned out to be the less important. They were merely *précis* of incoming telegrams, replies to which had been widely circulated. Any one of several State Department officials could have filched the memos and passed them to Chambers, who admitted having had other informants in the office. And the memos were of little Intelligence interest anyway.

But the typed documents appeared to bring treachery right inside the walls of the Hiss home. Alger Hiss had had official access to the originals. Experts testified that all but one of the sixty-five copies had been typed on the machine belonging to Priscilla Hiss. It seems to have been accepted by the court that Alger Hiss never used a typewriter. So the question appeared to be: Had Priscilla typed the copies during 1937 and 1938? Or had Chambers clandestinely typed them on the Hiss machine, either then or in later years? The possibility that someone else had got into the Hiss apartment and secretly used Priscilla's machine was too remote to be considered.

Priscilla denied, of course, having typed the documents. Copying even sixty-four sheets—presumably a selection from a greater number—would have taken a considerable time. Neighbours testified that they had never heard the sound of typing from the Hiss apartment for regular and prolonged periods; but the same neighbours said that they had been irritated by typewriter noises made by a later tenant who was a journalist. It tended to exonerate Priscilla.

So could Chambers have typed the copies on the Hiss machine? Some of the sheets contained columns of figures, the copying of which would have involved a good deal of time and care, especially for a non-professional typist. It seemed beyond the bounds of possibility that, during social visits by Mr and Mrs Chambers to Mr and Mrs Hiss, Chambers could have got through all that work in a small apartment without being detected and challenged.

The prosecution produced in court what they claimed to be the original Hiss typewriter, which had passed through a number of hands after having been given away when Priscilla acquired a new portable machine. Experts showed by enlarged photographs that certain typographical faults which had developed in the machine after years of wear and tear appeared to be identical in personal letters that were admittedly typed by Priscilla, in the Baltimore documents, and in a specimen typed in court on the alleged Hiss machine.

Handwriting experts can give an opinion as to whether two compared manuscript documents were written by the same individual. But comparison of greatly enlarged photographs of typed documents is not a matter of opinion but a matter of observable fact when a number of identical imperfections in the compared typescripts removes the question far beyond the possibilities of coincidence. A sheet of typescript is, in fact, as characteristic and identifiable as a human fingerprint.

It is a tribute to the integrity and intelligence of the jury at the first perjury trial—the jury that could not agree—that they clearly appreciated the vital importance of the Baltimore documents. As laymen they had little option but to accept—rightly or wrongly—the opinion of the experts that the copies had been typed on the Hiss machine. But during their retirement the jury considered an interesting point that had not been raised by the prosecution experts or the defence attorneys: Allowing that it was the same typewriter that had been used, was it the same hand that had used it?

I am not a typewriter expert, merely an Intelligence officer, but I know that the origin of illicit radio messages can be identified by what is called in Intelligence jargon the 'handwriting' in which a spy taps out messages on his Morse key. So it seems to me to be equally easy—if not easier—for a style of 'handwriting' to be detected in the approximate number of, say, 100,000 type impressions on sixty-four sheets of typescript. And the amateurish bashing of the keys by Priscilla Hiss would be more likely to show identifiable irregularities, such as varying pressures and over-typings, than the work of a trained touch-typist.

In an effort to settle this point the first jury sent for the typewriter produced in court and made their own experiments on it, disregarding, as juries do so often and so rightly, the opinions of the experts. They eventually disagreed by eight votes against Hiss and four in his favour, and a second trial was ordered.

There seems little doubt that the jury at the second trial pounced on and accepted the typewriter identification as the one piece of apparently irrefutable evidence in a wearying maze of irreconcilable contradictions. And they found that in denying that he had been a Soviet agent Hiss had been guilty of perjury before the grand jury. He was sentenced to five years' imprisonment; an appeal failed; and, officially, that was the end of the case of Alger Hiss.

VI

As well as many shorter pieces at least five lengthy books have been written about the case of Alger Hiss: *In the Court of Public Opinion*, by Hiss himself; *Witness*, by Whittaker Chambers; *The Strange Case of Alger Hiss*, by the Earl Jowitt, England's former Lord Chancellor; *A Generation on Trial*, by Alistair Cooke; and *Seeds of Treason* by Toledano and Lasky. So there is little I can add in the way of comment except on two points, which do not prove Hiss innocent or guilty, but which might possibly have affected the outcome of the case.

Firstly, although I have had a long and wide experience of court tactics in British criminal cases, it might seem presumptuous of me as a layman to criticize the tactics of so brilliant a lawyer as Alger Hiss. But it must be remembered that he had always been a back-room boy, accustomed to reflection in a quiet office rather than to the rough-and-tumble of the courts. So let me say that I think it was ill-advised of him under cross-examination to take advantage of repeated and admittedly tempting opportunities to score off the prosecuting attorney. Purely as a matter of tactics, it is much safer for a witness to adopt an attitude of puzzled but anxious-to-be-helpful innocence rather than one of I-can-beat-you-at-your-own-game smart-aleckry.

For instance, Hiss was asked about a debt which Chambers might have owed him. "You'd have ran after him for that?" queried the attorney. "I would have run after him," agreed Hiss, gently correcting his opponent's shaky grammar. "You didn't mean to correct me that way, did you?" asked the exasperated attorney. "I was testifying in my normal speech," replied Hiss. The implication was obvious.

In connection with the gift to Hiss of a rug (part payment of rent, said Hiss; but, a token of gratitude from Russian spy-master Colonel Bykov, said Chambers), Hiss said that Chambers came to the door of the Hiss apartment with the rug over his arm. He could not remember after all those years whether or not he opened the door to Chambers himself. "I thought you said he came to the door?" queried the attorney. "That is the way he entered the house," replied Hiss, which rocked the court with laughter.

And again about the rug, the attorney asked whether, when Chambers appeared, Hiss "implied" that the rug was in part payment of money owing. "I think he implied it; I inferred it," smiled Hiss, whose highly trained mind worked more quickly and accurately than his opponent's.

In those examples, among others, of verbal cut-and-thrust, I cannot help feeling that Hiss won the laughter but lost the sympathy of the court. Starting from the basis that Chambers, a self-confessed traitor and double-crosser, had made sensational accusations against Hiss, a brilliant man with an unblemished record of public service, I think that impulsive public sympathy for a good man accused by a bad man might have created an atmosphere initially favourable to Hiss, in spite of improper newspaper comment.

But Hiss made what I believe to have been the tactical error of showing the court not that he was an innocent citizen harried by Government attorneys with all the resources of the State behind them, not even that he was as good a lawyer as his adversaries, but that he was their intellectual—and even grammatical—superior. Hiss was right, of course, but even at this distance of time and space I seem to sense a certain illogical sympathy in court for the maddened attorney when Hiss repeatedly underlined his misuse of the English language.

There was a small detail of the evidence which nobody seems previously to have realized was mishandled by the defence. Its possible significance could not be appreciated, of course, without some knowledge of Soviet Secret Service methods. There were arguments as to whether or not Chambers had collected Communist Party subscriptions from Alger and Priscilla Hiss. All Intelligence officers who have studied Soviet methods as long as I have known that, for obvious reasons, their agents are strictly forbidden to pay Party dues and thus get their names into Party records which might be seized by counter-espionage officers. So the paradoxical position arose that a good defence against the accusation of having been a Soviet spy would have been for Hiss to produce a Party card showing that his subscriptions were paid up to date! That should have disposed of the treason charge, compared with which a charge of Communist sympathies would have been relatively insignificant.

VII

From the solitude of his cell in the Federal Penitentiary at Lewisburg, Pennsylvania, Alger Hiss urged his lawyers to continue the fight to clear his name.

The appeal having failed, they were entitled to apply for a fresh trial if there were grounds for stating that new evidence had come to light; but that had to be done within two years of judgment having been given. And after protracted and difficult investigations new evidence *was* found—not merely new but quite sensational evidence. The application for a fresh trial was made with one day to spare within the two year limit.

This new evidence related to the identification of the Woodstock typewriter produced in court (let us call it the court machine) and the Woodstock typewriter which had belonged to Priscilla Hiss (let us call it the Hiss machine). It was now claimed that these were two different machines, the former having been 'doctored' to reproduce the type-style and typographical faults of the latter.

The investigations of the Hiss lawyers were difficult because, during over twenty years since the machine had been manufactured, some commercial records had been destroyed and some had been impounded by the FBI. And, in view of the strong feelings engendered by the Hiss trial, several witnesses whose evidence might have helped Hiss refused to make affidavits to his lawyers, "for fear of personal consequences", as one of them put it. American public opinion of the day was apt to brand as a fellow-traveller anyone who lifted a finger to help a 'Commie'. ("Imagine," remarked an official at UNO headquarters in Washington, "the embarrassment of all the people here whom Alger Hiss recommended for their jobs!")

The history of the Hiss machine, as far as it could be traced, was that it had originally belonged to the father of Priscilla Hiss, Mr Fansler, who had been a Philadelphia insurance broker. When he retired he gave to it his daughter, and it was in her possession by 1933. Some years later—the date could not be established—she gave it to her coloured maid for her two teenage sons. Both Alger and Priscilla Hiss testified that they had bought a new portable machine in the autumn of 1937, and it may be thought reasonable to assume that the old machine was given away not long afterwards. That would have been nearly a year before the end of the period during which Priscilla was supposed to have been using the machine to copy documents for Whittaker Chambers.

In the maid's home the boys and their friends gave the Hiss machine some rather rough treatment, and it appears that at teenage parties it was regarded as great fun to bash away at the old typewriter. Then the boys' sister took it to the home of a doctor for whom she worked, and later left it to be taken over by her successor. Someone else took it away when the doctor died, and gave it to a removal man in part payment for a job. He in turn gave it to his daughter, who tried to learn typing on it, apparently without much success. Then her brother took it—"It was in such bad condition", he said—for his little girl to play with. It seems surprising that after all that the poor old machine was capable, years later, of functioning at all. But an FBI agent was able to copy a document on the machine produced in court.

The Hiss lawyers examined the court machine and noted the manufacturer's serial number, No. 230,099. Woodstock company records showed that it was probably manufactured during August 1929, and could not possibly have been manufactured earlier than the first week in July 1929. But Mr Fansler's machine was in use in his office at least as early as July 8th, 1929. Would it have been possible for No. 230,099 to be made, sold to the wholesalers, sold by them to the retailers, and sold by them to Mr Fansler within a week? It must have been quick work.

Examination of the court machine's typefaces showed that they were of an obsolete style, used by the Woodstock company from 1926 to 1928, and just possibly during the early weeks of 1929—not, it appears, on machines made in July or August 1929, as No. 230,099 had been.

So the Hiss lawyers felt it reasonable to suggest that—

although there was a narrow margin in the matter of dates—the Hiss machine and the court machine were not identical. The implication of an elaborate and sinister 'frame-up' by parties unknown was sensational.

Prosecution experts at the trial, however, had shown that the style and imperfections of the typefaces were identical in Priscilla's private letters, in the Baltimore documents, and in the specimen typed in court. The evidence seemed conclusive.

But the Hiss lawyers would not give up. They insisted—and, it may be agreed, not without justification—that typefaces on the Hiss machine which had become largely obsolete by late 1928, and certainly by early 1929, could not possibly have been soldered at the factory on to the type-bars of a machine which could not have been made before July 1929.

The only possible explanation of these discrepancies, said the Hiss lawyers and their experts, was that No. 230,099 had had its proper typefaces removed and replaced by obsolete typefaces to match those on the older Hiss machine, and that these had been skilfully doctored to reproduce the imperfections which specimen documents showed to have developed with wear and tear on the Hiss machine typefaces. I have closely examined enlarged photographs of the soldering of typefaces to type-bars on No. 230,099 and a 'control' machine of comparable age. It certainly appears that the workmanship on the former is fairly neat but variable, whereas the workmanship in the latter—the normal factory soldering—is much neater and completely uniform.

But despite these facts, which were not available at the trial, the motion for a fresh trial for Alger Hiss was rejected. He served his sentence and, since his release, has continued the fight to establish his innocence.

VIII

Of the host of unanswerable questions which arise from the case of Alger Hiss, that which overshadows all others is, of course: Was it Hiss or was it Chambers who was guilty of what Earl Jowitt called "massive and monumental lying"?

If Hiss were guilty it is understandable that he should lie like the Devil to save his skin and protect his family from social and economic ruin. But in that case it is impossible to understand why a man of such high intelligence, and in a position where a hint of treachery could—and, in fact, did—hit the headlines overnight, omitted the most elementary precautions to protect himself. Why, if he knew that Chambers was a Soviet agent, did he let him call so regularly at his home, possibly watched by nosy neighbours from behind their window-curtains? Why did he let Priscilla copy borrowed secret documents on her own identifiable typewriter? Why, after Chambers said he had photographed the typescripts, did Hiss not demand them back so that he could be sure of their destruction by burning them himself? Why, after Chambers defected and the possibility of betrayal arose, was the identifiable Hiss machine casually given away to a traceable witness instead of being irrecoverably dumped in the Potomac river? Hiss was not, after all, a novice in elementary security precautions.

If, on the other hand, Hiss were innocent, why should he have been chosen as the victim of a Machiavellian 'frame-up' plot—a plot involving the patient doctoring of the faked typewriter No. 230,099—a plot requiring original State Department documents (presumably borrowed by an agent as well placed in the Department as himself) so that they could be typed on the sheets which did so much to incriminate Hiss—a plot which, if Chambers were the instigator and master-mind, he concealed when he defected from the Soviet Secret Service in 1938, concealed when he made statements to the FBI in 1938 and again in 1945, concealed when he was subpoenaed to appear before the House Committee in 1948, and first brought to light when he was sued for slander?

If Hiss were guilty the anger of the Russians could be understood when he deserted them. But would they wait ten years before punishing him? Normally they act very promptly; in a near-parallel case they arranged for Dr Fuchs to be arrested as soon as he refused to work for them any more.[1]

And, in any case, surely there would have been some simpler and more certain way of framing Hiss than what must have been, if his lawyers' theory be accepted, one of the most elaborate of such schemes ever devised, comparable only with the simpler Hitler-Stalin plot to forge the documents which took Marshal Tukachevsky down into the Lubianka shooting-cellars.

As a Scotsman I say without hesitation that in my native country the verdict in the strange case of Alger Hiss would have been: Not Proven.

[1] See *Spy Mysteries Unveiled*, previously quoted.